A Book Full of Pages

A BOOK FULL OF PAGES

Penelope S Whitney

To Steve,
with all good
wishes from
Penny

First published in Great Britain in 2019 by

Escritor Publishing Services
34 Gallows Drive
Ferndown BH22 8RJ

ISBN 978-1-9161933-0-7

Typeset in Palatino Linotype
Printed and bound by CMP-UK Ltd, Poole

escritor
PUBLISHING

For Catherine

CONTENTS

    The Scott Family
    The Page and Retemeyer Cousins
    Samuel Page 1796-1860

Introduction

MANY EVENTS TOOK place in 1888, some of national importance and some purely of familial significance. In this year the first roll film camera, a Kodak, was patented in the US. In Germany Queen Victoria's grandson became Wilhelm II, Emperor of Germany and King of Prussia and known eventually as "Kaiser Bill". In England five young women lost their lives to the notorious serial killer, Jack the Ripper. In Milwaukee, Wisconsin, Samuel Page the Younger donated a painting to the newly opened Frederick Layton Art Museum. In Adelaide, Australia, it was the start of the Page vs Page court case which continued for 29 years and is the main subject of this book. And importantly for me, my grandfather William Augustus Page was born in Quetta, India.

This grandfather, William Augustus Page, died in Harrow, Middlesex, before I was born. I was told that he was an orphan. I knew that he had been in the cavalry in the first world war. He was a Squadron Quartermaster Sergeant in the King Edward's Horse. He married my grandmother and they had two sons, Douglas and Roy. His occupation was a timber merchant and he lived in true suburbia, South Harrow, in north west London. It was also understood within the family that he had no liking for the Freemason organisation, although there were two sets of Freemason aprons and sashes within his possessions. This was more or less the only information I had about my grandfather. I was intrigued to find out who his parents were. There was no information about them in the slim folder of Page family information and photographs. Just a couple of photographs with annota-

1

tions to 'dear cousin Willie' from 'Uncle Harry'. And I had no idea who he was, either.

I did know my grandfather's parents' names, because they were on his birth certificate. His father was William Augustus Page, a Colour Sergeant in the Kings Own Yorkshire Light Infantry, and his mother was Mary Anne (née Briggs). I had searched for quite a long time, unsuccessfully, on various census records to find more information about these great-grandparents. One evening, when I typed both their names into a search engine a website popped up listing their marriage. This was in Malta! I was amazed.

The website listed their marriage at St Paul's pro-Cathedral in Valletta, Malta in November 1885. Mary Anne's father, Robert Denny Briggs was a master tailor in an army regiment also stationed in Malta and was a witness at their wedding. So, William and Mary Anne had met at the garrison, at Verdala, courted and married. In August 1886 Mary Anne gave birth to their daughter, Edith Frances Elizabeth. The regiment was then deployed to India and set sail for Karachi in February 1887. Their final destination was the Army cantonment at Quetta. It was a major defence garrison, defending the border with Afghanistan after the Anglo-Afghan war of 1879. Soon their second child was on its way and in the fullness of time a son, William Augustus, my grandfather, named after his father, was born on 17th April 1888. The next day his father died. He was 28 years old.

One can only imagine Mary Anne's state of mind. To have given birth to a longed-for son and then to have lost her husband the next day. Poor woman. Fortunately, her father and his wife Elizabeth were also at Quetta cantonment, so I am sure that they were a great support to her. And for sure she needed their support, because three weeks later on 8th May her twenty-month old daughter, Edith, died of infantile convulsions. However, Mary Anne soldiered on with her new-born son and he was developing well and growing strong. Tragedy seemed to be behind them. In October he was 6 months old and beginning to be weaned. There were more than 1,000 British army personnel and their families stationed in the Quetta fort. In that era there were no antibiotics or other types of medicine that we take for granted these days; any infectious diseases spread like wildfire. Enteric fever, more commonly known as Typhoid, took hold in the cantonment and unfortunately Mary Anne succumbed on 13th October. William Augustus Page aged 6 months was all alone in the world, and a very long way from his home country.

One pressing question I'd always had was "how did he get to England from India if he was an orphan"? All the information about Malta and Quetta I have found out since I have been researching my family history. I am sure that my father would have been stunned to know that his grandparents had married in Malta. Dad knew nothing about his father's antecedents. He would be so amazed at what I have discovered!

Census searches are often the first port of call to find a lost relative. And so, it transpired. The 1891 census located William Augustus Page, aged 3, in Manningham Barracks, Bradford, with his grandfather Robert Denny Briggs and his wife Elizabeth and also his uncle Harry, aged 23. Harry was Mary Anne's brother. This was the 'Uncle Harry' whose little messages on photographs I had seen in the family archive. Robert is listed as a pensioner in the Durham Light Infantry. Some small family 'legends' such as 'his people came from the North' were beginning to ring true. The next census has William Augustus in the London Orphan Asylum, in Watford but lists him as being born in Newcastle upon Tyne. This was evidently incorrect and showed me, for the first but not the last time, that 'official' records are sometimes wrong. I later discovered that grandfather Robert Briggs died in 1904, the same year that William Augustus Page left the orphanage at age 15.

Now that I had discovered that his maternal grandfather brought him back to England, I became curious about his paternal grandparents. If they existed why hadn't they helped take care of him? Why was he in an orphanage?

I knew from his parent's wedding certificate from the army in Malta, that his father was born in Godalming, Surrey. From that information I was able to track down his paternal grandfather. He too was William Augustus Page. Sometimes it is good to have the same names, as you know you have the 'right' people. This grandfather William Augustus Page, my great-great grandfather, was a provision merchant. He had died in 1896, when William, known by Uncle Harry as Willie, was only 8 years old. It seems that Willie entered the orphanage at around that time. Grandfather William Augustus had been born in Wandsworth, London, in 1835 and his father was called Samuel Page.

At last – another name in the Page family! At this stage I had no idea that Samuel Page would lead me on an amazing journey, literally to the other side of the world. Samuel Page had seven children, whom you will read about later. As already stated, he had one son called William Augustus Page, one grandson called William Augustus Page, who died in India, and a great-grandson called William Augustus Page. Later on, I discovered another two grandsons named William Augustus Page! It was confusing for me, so dear reader it is probably confusing for you too. Please refer to the family tree to keep track.

PART 1

Samuel Page's Family

Chapter 1

Samuel Page

SAMUEL WAS THE youngest of the three children of John and Elizabeth Page. His sister Jane was born in 1790 and his brother John three years later. Their father, John, died in 1797 aged 32. Samuel was just one year old. John Page was a livery stable keeper and left a Will but was not a wealthy man. His Will starts "In the name of God herein, I John Page of Clapham in the County of Surrey, stable keeper, being weak of body but of sound mind and memory do dispose of my effects…".

He left £300 in 3 per cent Consolidated to be invested towards the upkeep of his wife and children. I guess that £9 per annum was not very much with which to raise a family, so on 16th June 1800 Elizabeth married again, to Thomas Sessions. Thomas was an ostler, so probably he had been employed by John Page at the livery stable. They weren't married at Holy Trinity, Clapham, which is where they lived, but at St Bride's on Fleet Street, north of the River. The fact that a daughter, Mary, was born a month later, 20th July, may have had something to do with it.

Elizabeth and Thomas had three more children: William, a son, who died aged 7 in 1810, and two more daughters; Ann, born 1805, and Elizabeth, who arrived in 1807. Elizabeth had six living children when her second husband, Thomas, died in 1814. He was only 39. Her eldest daughter Jane was married that same year to William Beech, and they set up home on their own. Samuel had been apprenticed in 1810, when he was 14 years old, to Alexander

Sinclair Gordon of Fish Street Hill in the City of London. Apprenticeships in those days lasted for 7 years, so at 21 you were skilled in your trade, which entitled Samuel to become a Freeman of the City of London, in Goldsmith's Livery Company. Alexander Sinclair Gordon was an oil merchant. This was in the days of oil lamps, and oil came from whaling, amongst other natural sources – not oil from the ground, which is how we understand oil and petroleum products in the 21at century.

Samuel's maternal grandparents were George Scott, of Leeds, but who was a victualler and vintner in Clapham, Surrey, and Jane, née Thompson. As well as their daughter Elizabeth, they were the parents of Thompson, born 1772, and Jane who arrived in 1776.

At some stage in his youth, Samuel was living with his uncle Thompson Scott at Brabant Court on Philpot Lane, City of London. The building is still there and lies just beneath the Sky Building, also known as the 'walkie talkie'. I assume that his uncle took him in, as his mother, having several children, would be struggling without a husband. Her siblings were very helpful to Elizabeth; not only did Thompson take Samuel to live with him, her sister Jane took Samuel's younger half-sisters, Ann and Elizabeth, to live with her in Arbroath, Scotland, with her husband, Adam Kirkaldy, a farmer.

Thompson Scott died in 1817 in Nice, France, where he had gone for the sake of his health. His very interesting Will gives the main beneficiary, after numerous bequests, as Samuel Page! In fact, Thompson Scott had a 'natural daughter' called Clara, who was born in 1811 and lived in Clapham. She was provided for in Thompson's Will, but I discovered that she died in 1825 aged 14.

So, in 1818 Samuel had come into money and completed his apprenticeship. What next? Marriage of course! On the 30th April 1923 Samuel married Mary Ann Stonehouse at St Mary's Lambeth. Mary Ann was a twin and her sister was called Mary. Their mother was also called Mary. How very confusing!

Any references to Samuel that I have found, give his occupation as Provision Merchant. His uncle, Thompson Scott, started the business in 1805. In due course this business became 'Samuel Page and Son' and lasted until the 1990s. The offices of the company at that time were at 5 Catherine Court, Water Street, Tower Hill, City of London. The Port of London Authority building is now on that site.

Samuel and Mary Ann settled down at Priory, Wandsworth Road, South Lambeth. Children came thick and fast:

Thompson Scott Page, 1824

Samuel Page, 1825

Mary Ann Page, 1827

Eliza Page, 1829

Adam Kirkaldy Page, 1831

James Stonehouse Page, 1833

William Augustus Page, 1836

Adelaide Page, 1838

Apart from James Stonehouse, who died aged 6, all the other children lived to adulthood.

Adam Kirkaldy, the farmer uncle in Arbroath Scotland, died in 1836. Samuel Page was the joint executor/trustee, together with a nephew of Adam's, George Kirkaldy. Samuel and George were joint beneficiaries after various other bequests. Samuel had done very well financially from both his uncles.

What to do with some of the money? A good investment was needed, especially with so many children. At about this time the 'Wakefield' scheme was mooted whereby investors could invest in non-convict settlements in Australia. With the invested money the Government would supply labour, in the shape of assisted passages to the colony for single men and young married couples who wanted a new start, away from England and unemployment. And, so it was that the city of Adelaide was founded, marked out into one-acre town lots and 134-acre country lots. Samuel Page purchased Land Order 51 on 16th December 1835 for £81. This entitled him to a town acre and a 134-acre country section, selected by ballot. His ballot was the 26th when the draw took place on 28th March 1837. His town acre was number 335 and his country section was Goodwood Section 8.

However, his investment in land in Adelaide did not go entirely as he had planned. The Government reneged on their side of the bargain and after initial subsidised passages they withheld the invested monies. I found some fascinating correspondence between Samuel Page and Lord Stanley, the Foreign and Colonial Secretary. Lord Stanley later became Prime Minister – and was then known as the Earl of Derby. This was reported in the Australian press, at the time.

From the South Australian, 28th March 1845
THE EMIGRATION FUND

> We lately gave a summary from the South Australian News of the contents of the papers relating to above fund, furnished to Parliament on the motion of Mr Divett. Having published papers now before us, we propose to copy the greater part at length for public edification. We commence with the correspondence of Mr Page with Lord Stanley, part of which only was given in the summary. Everyone must admit that this correspondence is most instructive, and most creditable to Mr Page:

> Culloden House
> Wandsworth Road
> March 9, 1844

> My Lord – Being deeply interested in the prosperity of South Australia, having land and other property in that interesting and thriving colony, and as one of my sons may eventually go out and settle as a farmer, must plead my excuses for taking the liberty of thus addressing your Lordship.

> For some time past, all the accounts received from South Australia, both from private sources and the official dispatched of Governor Grey, state that the great impediment

10

to any further advancement of the colony, is the great want of labour, and that it is even doubtful whether it will be possible to obtain sufficient hands to secure the harvest of 1843; the quantity of land under cultivation having considerably increased since the previous year, when it was with the greatest difficulty that the crops could be got in, even with the assistance of the military, and of everybody that could be spared from the town.

Under these circumstances, as your reply to several communications and deputations that have waited on your Lordship has been, that you are willing to resume emigration to South Australia as soon as you were in possession of funds applicable to that purpose, I beg respectfully to call your Lordship's attention to the circumstances that £8,000 was paid by Colonel Gawler about the year 1840, into the Bank of South Australia to the credit of her Majesty's Colonisation Commissioners for South Australia, being the proceeds of land sales, to be expressly devoted to emigration. This amount, which, with accumulations, will now have increased to near £10,000 was demanded from the bank at Adelaide by Governor Grey, but payment was refused, instructions having been sent from the directors in London not to pay the money without an order being produced from your Lordship; therefore, as the demand for emigration is now urgent, and there is a fund lying in the hand of the South Australian Banking Company in London expressly applicable to this purpose, I would suggest that the money should be applied for and devoted to its legitimate object, being convinced that nothing will tend so much to relieve this colony from the difficulties which it has so nobly struggled to overcome, as a fresh supply of labour to enable the settlers more fully to develop its resources.

I have, etc.

Samuel Page (Signed)

Copy of Letter from G W Hope Esq to Samuel Page Esq
Downing Street
16th March 1844
Sir – Lord Stanley directs me to acknowledge the receipt of

your letter of the 9th instant, and to acquaint you that it has been referred for the consideration and report of the Commissioners of Colonial Land and Emigration.

I am etc.

G W Hope (signed)

Copy of Letter from Samuel Page Esq to G W Hope Esq

Culloden House,
Wandsworth Road
3rd April 1844

My Lord – I was favoured with your letter of the 16th ultimo, in reply to my communication respecting the Emigration Fund due from the South Australian Banking Company.

Your Lordship referred me to the Colonial Land and Emigration Commissioners, who have informed me that they have reported on the subject to your Lordship, and again refer me to you.

I shall therefore feel much obliged for a reply to my inquiry (at your earliest convenience) whether this money is available for the purpose of renewed emigration to South Australia.

I have, etc.

Samuel Page (signed)

Copy of Letter from G W Hope Esq to Samuel Page Esq

Downing Street
April 4, 1844

Sir – With reference to my letter of the 16th ultimo, I am directed by Lord Stanley to acquaint you that his Lordship does not consider it necessary to pursue any further the discussion of the question raised by your letter of the 9th ultimo.

I have, etc.

G W Hope (signed)

Copy of Letter from Samuel Page Esq to G W Hope Esq
Culloden House,
Wandsworth Road
25th April 1844

My Lord – I am in receipt of Mr Hope's letter of the 4th instant, in reply to my application to your Lordship respecting the money due to the emigration Fund of South Australian from the South Australian Banking Company (say £8,000) in which he states "that your Lordship does not consider it necessary to pursue any further discussion of the question raised by my letter of the 9th ultimo."

I would, however, observe, that as a holder of land in the colony, purchased under the guarantee of an act of Parliament, that the whole of the proceeds should be appropriated to emigration; and as the accounts recently received state, that there is a greater demand than ever for labour, and that some farmers had even preferred the entire loss of their crops rather than pay the exorbitant rates demanded for reaping, and also that land has no marketable value, solely for want of labour to bring it into cultivation.

I therefore ask, as a matter of justice to myself and others who have invested their capital in land in South Australia, that the above-mentioned money should be appropriated to its legitimate purpose.

I do not wish your Lordship to make any advances on account of the colony, but simply to apply the funds paid to the South Australian Banking Company for the specific object of emigration, to that purpose, by doing which you will confer a blessing on a colony which has shown its capability of production, by exporting, in the seventh year of its existence, considerable quantities of wheat to this country, besides what has been shipped to neighbouring colonies, and which might be annually much increased, were there but labour to further develop its resources.

I have etc.

Samuel Page (Signed)

Copy of Letter from G W Hope Esq to Samuel Page Esq
Downing Street
May 4th, 1844

Sir – I am directed by Lord Stanley to acknowledge the receipt of your letter of the 25th ultimo, and to refer you to my letter of the 4th ultimo, as containing the only answer which Lord Stanley can return to your present communication.

I am, etc.

G W Hope (Signed)

Copy of Letter from Samuel Page Esq to G W Hope Esq
Culloden House,
Wandsworth Road
May 10, 1844

My Lord – Having, upon the faith of an Act of Parliament, passed the 15th August 1834, in the fourth year of the reign of William IV, purchased land in South Australia, upon the distinct representation that the whole of the purchase money was to be appropriated in sending out agricultural and other labour, I shall feel very much obliged in being informed by your Lordship whether the £56,000 due to the Emigration Fund is to be appropriated to its legitimate purpose, now being the time to send out labour, which, from accounts, recently received, is so much wasted in that thriving and interesting colony; but in case this fund is not to be applied in the way as was originally intended , I should wish to have my money (from the Commissioners) returned, and I think I am also entitled to receive interest from the time I paid for the said land, which I consider to be totally valueless, without labour.

I have, etc.

Samuel Page (Signed)

Copy of Letter from Samuel Page Esq to G W Hope Esq
Culloden House,
Wandsworth Road
May 29, 1844

My Lord – I had the honour to address your Lordship the 10th instant, and not having had a reply, I have an idea that my letter has not been delivered.

I therefore now (for particular reasons) enclose a copy addressed to your private residence and shall feel much obliged by a reply at your earliest convenience.

The present is not a political question; I am a decided supporter of the present Government, and a member of the Goldsmith's Company.

I have etc.

Samuel Page (Signed) [*vide* above]

Copy of Letter from G W Hope Esq to Samuel Page Esq
Downing Street
June 4, 1844

Sir – I am directed by Lord Stanley to acknowledge the receipt of your letters of the 10th and 29th May last, and to acquaint you that on the 17th of that month the first of these letters was referred, by his Lordship's direction, to the Colonial Land and Emigration Commissioners, with whom it still remains.

I am etc.

G W Hope (Signed)

Copy of Letter from G W Hope Esq to Samuel Page Esq
Downing Street
June 11, 1844

Sir – With reference to my letter of the 4th instant, I am directed by Lord Stanley to acquaint you that his lordship cannot authorise a compliance with your application for the repayment of the purchase money which you paid some years ago for land in South Australia, and which land was consequently conveyed to you.

I am etc.

G W Hope (Signed)

Copy of Letter from Samuel Page Esq to G W Hope Esq
Culloden House,
Wandsworth Road
June 28, 1844

My Lord – I was favoured with Mr Hope's reply of the 11th instant, to my application to your Lordship respecting the repayment of the money paid for land purchased in South Australia, in default of its being appropriated to emigration.

Mr Hope states that your Lordship cannot sanction the repayment of that purchased, because the land had been conveyed to me; but this, I must beg to observe is only one part of the contact, it being expressly provided by Act of Parliament, that the whole of such funds should be appropriated to emigration; and as my land is now worthless, without a supply of labour to bring it into cultivation, I request, as a matter of right and justice, either that the whole of the original contract be performed, or else that my money may be returned, on receipt of which I will reconvey the land allotted to me.

I have etc,

Samuel Page (Signed)

Copy of Letter from G W Hope Esq to Samuel Page Esq
Downing Street
July 4, 1844

Sir – I am directed by Lord Stanley to acknowledge the receipt of your letter of the 28th ultimo, renewing your application for repayment of the money laid out by you some years ago, in the purchase of land in South Australia; and his Lordship desires me, in reply, to acquaint you that it is wholly out of his power to comply with your request.

I am etc.

G W Hope (Signed)

Copy of Letter from Samuel Page Esq to G W Hope Esq
Culloden House,
Wandsworth Road
July 6, 1844

My Lord – Since I had the honour of addressing your Lordship, the 28th ultimo, I find in the last Blue Book, published by the House of Commons, on South Australia, the following extract of a letter (page 48) from T. Fred. Elliott and Edward E. Villiers, to James Stephen, Esq.:

"The amount due to the Emigration Fund, which the Committee recommend should be made good, was £56,000. It may be remarked, that of this sum, £24,600 is the extent to which specific individuals, as was explained in the evidence before the Committee (page 176), have a right to expect that emigrants should be sent out, if named by them in virtue of purchases which they made of land. The balance is due to emigration purposes, under the general system on which the colony was founded."

I feel confident, in my own mind, that if your Lordship was only to propose in the House of Commons the application of this money to its legitimate purposes, that there would not be the least opposition; on the contrary, I shall expect some morning on my arrival in the city, to read in the newspapers that you have done so. The sum of £24,600 relates to my own case.

I have, etc.

Samuel Page (Signed)

Copy of Letter from Samuel Page Esq to G W Hope Esq
Culloden House,
Wandsworth Road,
July 13, 1844

My Lord – I have to acknowledge the receipt of Mr Hope's letter of the 9th instant, in reply to mine of the 28th ult., to your Lordship.

If I had received such a reply from a private individual, instead of a powerful Government, I should certainly have commenced an action for breach of contract. Referring to my letter of the 6th instant,

I have etc.

Samuel Page (Signed)

Well Samuel, that was telling Lord Stanley, wasn't it? No doubt it left you feeling satisfied that you had vented your spleen on his Lordship, but unfortunately, I do not think it had any effect on his ability to release the funds that you so badly wanted to ensure that your lands in Australia could be put to profitable use.

NB. G W Hope was secretary to Lord Stanley. Lord Stanley was, at this time, Colonial Secretary in Sir Robert Peel's government.

Chapter 2

A Son in Adelaide

SAMUEL PAGE WROTE to the Foreign and Colonial Secretary, Lord Stanley, in 1844 about the Government not fulfilling their part of the contract of development of South Australia. They refused to pay for assisted passages to Adelaide for young men and women, in search of an adventure and a new life in Australia. I do not know if anything was officially done about the Government reneging on their side of the agreement. I think it is not difficult to appreciate the frustration that Samuel Page was feeling, as his investment was not fulfilling his expectations.

Samuel Page attended a couple of 'South Australian Soirée's during 1848 and 1849. Also attending were John Hutt, late Governor of Western Australia, Colonel Gawler, Captain Sturt, G F Angas, Mr & Mrs Morphett, D McLaren Manager of the South Australian Banking Company, and other people who can still be identified on streets named after them in Adelaide today. Perhaps Samuel had discussions with these eminent people about the current situation. I feel sure that he did.

In Samuel's correspondence to Lord Stanley he mentioned that he had a son who might go out to South Australia to farm. I was surprised by this, because although Lambeth and Clapham were relatively outside of the centre of London, I don't believe that they were farming territory, even in the 1840s. However, his eldest son, Thompson Scott Page, did set sail for Adelaide in 1849.

What was Adelaide like, what would he find when he arrived there? Would it be very different from the metropolis of London? The population of Adelaide at the 1851 census was 14,577. Copper, copper ore, wheat, flour and wool were the main exports. In the third quarter of 1850 exports were valued at £81,000, whereas imports amounted to £269,000. Most of the exports went to England. The South Australian colonists were to a great degree dependent on the steadiness of the markets in the mother country, so they were virtually at the mercy of brokers, merchants and manufacturers 12,000 miles away.

The Adelaide races were held on New Year's Day 1850. There followed four days of frivolity, excitement and boozing, with an occasional horse race to interrupt the fun.

In 1850 there were 88 hotels in Adelaide! Some of them may have been genteel establishments, but most would have sold grog. This number of hostelries might go some way to explain the first time that I managed to encounter Thompson Scott Page in Adelaide.

South Australian Register, Adelaide, Saturday 22nd December 1849

THOMPSON SCOTT PAGE

Henry Valette Jones came up on remand, charged with drunkenness and indecent behaviour, in Currie Street, between 4 and 5 o'clock on Tuesday morning.

His Worship – I adjourned the case to allow your witnesses time to attend. Are they in attendance?

Defendant – Yes sir. He then called Thompson Scott Page who described himself as a gentleman and stated that he was with the defendant when he was taken into custody. Mr Jones and a gentleman who had recently arrived from England were, with witness, returning from a party. Witness was a little in the rear. He saw Mr Jones standing with his face to the door of the 'Golden Fleece'. The police sergeant crossed the street and struck him, charging him with committing a wanton and unnecessary nuisance against the house door. He ordered Mr Jones to go home quietly, but irritated at being struck, he refused to do so, and was taken into custody. He (witness) believed the sergeant acted in consequence of what he said Mr Jones did. He (defendant) did not "let out a little" when he was struck.

The defendant admitted he was slightly intoxicated on the occasion.

His Worship – Then, if that is your only defence I consider the charged proved and you are fined £1.

The defendant was not in funds but was accommodated with the escort of a policeman in search of a friend in his need.

Not long after this court case there was an announcement in the Adelaide press:

Adelaide Times, Saturday 25 January 1851
PUBLIC NOTICE

Mr Thompson Scott Page having been appointed Agent for managing the property of his Father, Samuel Page Esq, of London, hereby gives notice that all rents are in future to be paid to him, his receipt being a sufficient discharge for the same.

NOTICE

The undersigned having been appointed by Osmond Arthur Wyatt Esq, of Monmouth, as agent for managing his property, requests that all rents are in future to be paid to him.

Thomson Scott Page - Exchange

Although Thompson Scott was 'netting' for his father it would appear that he was also trying to sell the land, although it was not his to sell. In addition to the land in Adelaide there were several parcels of land at Currency Creek, on the Fleurieu Peninsular, south of Adelaide.

Adelaide Times, Saturday 25 January 1851

For sale: Town Acre, No. 335, situate at the corner of Grote Street and Victoria Square, in the immediate proximity of the Government offices, New Post Office and Magistrate's Court, and within a short distance of the Court House, either in a single block, or in allotments to suit purchasers. For particulars apply between the hours of 11 and 2, to Thompson Scott Page at the Exchange.

To be let on lease: Several Agricultural Sections and Allotments of Land in different parts of the country. For particulars apply between the hours of 11 and 2, to Thompson Scott Page at the Exchange.

Adelaide Times, 24 October 1851

To be Sold: Nine sections on the River Murray, at Wellington and several other sections on the Light and Currency Creek. For particulars apply to Thompson Scott Page, South Terrace or at the Royal Exchange Hotel, Adelaide.

The next information about Thompson Scott was his wedding announcement to Helen Mansfield (née Best) of Crockenhill, Kent. Helen and Biggs Mansfield, a farmer, were married in Woolwich on 11th March 1850. I imagine that they were very likely a young couple who were encouraged to emigrate and possibly had their passage paid. Biggs' death is rather a mystery; perhaps he died on the sea voyage to Adelaide, or soon after they arrived. I haven't discovered any notice of his death.

So, I guess that Helen found herself another 'farmer'.

Adelaide Times, 22nd November 1851

Marriage – Mr Thompson Scott Page, Reed Beds, eldest son of Samuel Page Esq of London to Helen, widow of the late Biggs Mansfield, Esq.

Only one-month later Thompson Scott filed for bankruptcy, as recorded in the Adelaide newspaper.

South Australian Register, Wednesday 31 December 1851

Insolvency notices: Thompson Scott Page of Adelaide, farmer. Solicitor W Bakewell. Filed in court December 24th.

South Australian Register Saturday 9th October 1852
Insolvency Notices: Declaration of insolvency

Thompson Scott Page, of Goodwood, near Adelaide, gentleman

It was not long before Samuel Page, back in London, discovered the 'goings on' in South Australia and rescinded the right of Thompson Scott to collect his rents. The following notice appeared in the Adelaide press:

South Australian Register Wednesday 29th June 1853
Notice is hereby given that Samuel Page of No 5 Catherine Court, Tower Hill in the City of London, Esquire, hath, by an instrument bearing date the 5th February 1853 revoked and made void, so far as relates to Mr Thompson Scott Page, a certain power of attorney, bearing date the 16th September 1850, whereby he appointed Messrs William Snell Chauncy and Thompson Scott Page his attorneys joint and several for the purposes therein mentioned. And that the said Thompson Scott Page hath no longer any authority to net for the said Samuel Page.

Dated this twenty eighth day of June 1853, Bartley & Bakewell, Solicitors to the said Samuel Page.

And a few months later another announcement was made, appointing replacement agents to act on Samuel Page's behalf.

South Australian Register, Wednesday 9th November 1853
Notice is hereby given that Samuel Page of No 5 Catherine Court, Tower Hill in the City of London, merchant, has by Deed Poll, dated the 18th day of June 1853, under his hand and seal wholly revoked a certain Letter of Attorney, dated the 16th September 1850, whereby the said Samuel Page

appointed William Snell Chauncy and Thompson Scott Page his Attorneys, to act on his behalf within the province of South Australia and that the said Samuel Page has appointed James Walsh of Adelaide and George W Goyder of Adelaide his Attorneys, jointly and separately, to act for him in respect of his lands situate in Adelaide and elsewhere within the said province.

Dated 8th November 1853, Fenn & Wearing, Solicitors, Exchange Chambers.

Adelaide Observer, Saturday 4th February 1854
CLEARING OUT

Saturday 28th January – The barque 'Royal Shepherdess', 406 tons, ship's master Bell, bound for London.

Mr and Mrs Page and infant son plus 17 other persons in the cabins. 30 other persons in the intermediate.

So, Thompson and Helen Page were homeward bound to England, together with their son, also Thompson Scott Page, (the Younger) who was born 'on the Sturt' on 6th February 1853. The baby was thus almost a year old when they set sail. The voyage from Australia to England took about four months in those days, sometimes longer, depending on the winds. I wonder what reception they received when they arrived in London? Samuel was evidently not best pleased with Thompson's business activities in Adelaide, nor the fact that he was declared bankrupt.

There is no further information on Thompson Scott Page the Elder apart from the fact that he and Helen had two further sons: Alfred Samuel born 13th October 1855 and William Augustus on 3rd April 1857, both in Orpington, Kent. This was yet another William Augustus Page. In the 1871 census Thompson Scott Page senior was recorded as paralysed, living at Melrose Hall, Putney, Surrey, a home for incurables, where he died on 18th March 1872, aged 48. His death certificate described him as a farmer and the cause of death as heart disease and paralysis.

Chapter 3

Adam Kirkaldy Page

MEANWHILE, ADAM KIRKALDY Page, Samuel and Mary Ann Page's third son and fourth child, had set sail from England to Australia. He sailed from Liverpool on the *Nederwaard* a Dutch vessel of 565 tons. It is probably not co-incidental that Adam's mother's twin sister Mary lived in Liverpool. She had married Meinhard Retemeyer a Dutchman who had become a naturalised British citizen, and he was a merchant in that city.

The *Nederwaard* sailed from Liverpool on 28th January 1853, heading for Geelong, Melbourne and Adelaide, and the ship's master, Meyer, brought the ship into Port Adelaide on 27th May. It seems that Adam arrived in Adelaide a few months before his brother Thompson and Helen had decided to leave. However, I have no evidence that Adam was actually in Adelaide for any length of time, apart from the fact that the ship's manifest states that he disembarked there.

I did find Adam in Merimbula, NSW. In 2012, I contacted a genealogist, Pat Raymond, based in Pambula, NSW, who kindly undertook some research for me about Adam Kirkaldy Page. Pat was the Research Officer of the Bega Valley Genealogy Society. She spent many hours searching the local newspapers – which were not digitised online – and found him mentioned quite a lot. Some of her findings were advertisements for his business, therefore not very informative about Adam, but other information that she found was very enlightening. Here goes!

The first information I found online – not from Pat – was an article about Jellat. I reproduce part of it here. Adam was evidently a pioneer in the region.

> "Settlement of the Jellat area dates back to the 1850 period, when Ben Boyd, of Twofold Bay, Eden and Boydtown fame, established the Twofold Bay Pastoral Company, as one of his enterprises. This resulted in the setting up of the Warragaburra Station settlement a mile north-west of the present school site. On 25th February 1854 Assistant Surveyor Drake surveyed the first town (Bega) allotments. These were sold at Eden on 15th August 1854 at a price of £8 per acre. This land sale led to closer settlement in the area and resulted in the arrival of Jellat Jellat pioneers such as Daniel Gowing, W Manning, John McGregor, Meakers and Harts. These people were closely followed by William Hibburd, Robert Russell, Ritchies, Whiteleys, Johnstones, Watersons, Taylors, Connollys, Duncans, Simon Gordon and Adam Page. These pioneers were the ones destined to fashion farms from the wilderness and point the way for future development."

So, Adam was a pioneer in the region. In 1859 he was residing at Kameruka which was a large pastoral concern. Adam was the Storekeeper. At that time Kameruka was run by the Twofold Bay Pastoral Association. He was having his own store built in Merimbula, as this was the port where coastal ships called in. Adam's store opened on 1st September 1859 and at the same time he became the Shipping Agent for the Illawarra Steam Navigation Company. So, in a short space of time Adam had become the owner of a store and the agent for a large shipping company. And things got better, because in October the postmaster of Merimbula, Mr J S Kirkwood, wrote to the Postmaster General saying that he could no longer take on the responsibility of being postmaster and recommended that Adam Page take over the position. So, in November 1859 Adam became postmaster of Merimbula. Three jobs! He must have been very busy and probably wanted to share his burden. Sure enough, on the 14th December 1859, he got married.

His wife was Martha Rixon. Martha was the daughter of James Rixon and had 10 siblings. Born on 12th January 1806, James was one of two surviving brothers of the first white triplets born in Australia. His father, also James Rixon, was a convict. His story is interesting and probably reflects many of that time, when ne'er do wells and petty thieves were sent out to the colonies

It's believed the elder James Rixon was born about 1770. At the time of his conviction and sentencing, he was living in Ilkeston, a small market town in the Erewash Valley, Derbyshire, close to Nottinghamshire. At the Lent Assizes on 19 Mar 1792, the *Derby Mercury* reported the arrival of Sir Alexander Thomson, one of the Barons of his Majesty's Court of Exchequer, to hold the county assizes. There were only four prisoners, including James Hickson (later transposed to Rixon) aged 22, who was "Charged on the oath of William Reed on suspicion of privately stealing out of his box in the house of William Webster, of Ilkeston, on Monday the 24th of October last, the sum of Nine Guineas". The sentence "To be hang'd" was commuted to "transportation for life". Before transportation occurred, James spent five years on board the *Prudentia*, a prison hulk at Woolwich, Kent, where he worked at His Majesty's Dockyard, wearing leg irons. James Rixon eventually sailed to Australia, along with about 290 other convicts, leaving Portsmouth on November 7, 1797, aboard the *Barwell*. He was pardoned in 1801.

His son James was married to Elizabeth Hoare. James and Elizabeth's daughter Martha married Adam and several children were born during their marriage:

Adelaide Elizabeth Page, baptised 8 September 1861, Pambula Parish

Emily Page, baptised March 1864, Pambula Parish

Annie Rose Page, baptised 12 May 1865, Pambula Parish

William Augustus Page, baptised 9 May 1867, Pambula Parish

(This is the *third* William Augustus Page grandson for Samuel Page)

Francis Page, baptised 3 September 1869, Pambula Parish

Alice May Page, baptised 11 June 1872, Pambula Parish

Sadly, Emily died 2 July 1864 aged four months. She is buried at Bega Cemetery.

Going back to the start-up of Adam's business the following are two cuttings from the press at the time.

Illawarra Mercury, Thursday 25 August 1859

Mercantile Store, Merimbula, Twofold Bay

Adam K Page begs to inform the residents of Maneroo, Bega and the surrounding districts that he is about to open his extensive stores newly erected at Merimbula and that he will be fully prepared on the 1st September to offer all descriptions of goods at a very slight advance on Sydney prices, it being his determination to encourage the patronage of the public both by moderate prices and also by having only the best goods on his premises.

Illawarra Mercury, Thursday 1 September 1859

Illawarra Steamship Navigation Company - Residents at Maneroo, Bega and in the district of Twofold Bay are respectfully reminded that the first-class steam packets of the ISN Company leave Merimbula for Sydney at 12 o'clock every Tuesday and Sydney for Merimbula on each Saturday morning at 10 o'clock.

The arrangements for Merimbula are perhaps superior to any others in the colony – there being the means of landing or embarking an entire cargo, without risk of injury, in the short space of one hour, by means of a tramway from the ship's side to the centre of an extensive store, capable of containing several hundred bales of wool. The undersigned would attend to any instructions having reference to the receipt and shipment of goods, or the forwarding of emigrants to their destination. Adam K Page, Agent, Merimbula, Twofold Bay, 1 Sept 1859.

On the 20th January 1860 the *Illawarra Mercury* reports the arrival of a party at Bega. "Mr and Mrs Page of Merimbula Commercial Stores, accompanied by Mrs Rixon of Eden (mother of Mrs Page) arrived in the township last evening, on a visit to this locality, and put up at Mr John Needham's 'Family Hotel'. The two ladies, who have not been in Bega previously, are much pleased with the beauty of the landscape which is enhanced by the overwhelming amount of rain we have lately had in this place.

There are several reports in *Shipping Intelligence* of the goods that have arrived at Adam Page's Merimbula store. They are reported in the *Twofold Bay and Maneroo Telegraph*. A fairly typical report was on 16th September 1860 when the imports are listed as:

> 2 pole drays, 14 yokes and bows, 14 chains, 4 chests tea, 10 packages, timber 1510 feet, 9 cases, 1 qr cask wine, 3 bundles tarpaulins, 7 cases furniture, 15 bags flour, 5 mats sugar, 2 rolls matting, 2 bundles frying pans, 1 bundle spades, 1 truss, 1 cask, 1 cask earthenware, 1 keg, 1 box currants.

To modern readers, such an extraordinary list does emphasise how dependent folk were on very basic foodstuffs – there were no ready-meals or take-aways in that era! Soon after this the Postmaster General received a letter from Adam dated 24th September 1860:

> "Sir,
>
> I am sorry that in consequence of ill health I shall be reluctantly compelled to resign my office as Postmaster. I beg humbly to recommend Mr Bate of the firm of Berkelman and Bate, Millers of Merimbula, to act in my stead.
>
> I have the honour to be Sir,
>
> Your obedient servant, Adam K Page."

Adam had only been in the Postmaster role for one year. Perhaps ill-health had influenced his decision. My feeling is that because he was the agent for the Illawarra Steamship Navigation

Company as well as owning his own store and with the potential arrival of a baby the postmaster role was too much, and he wanted to divest it to someone else.

His store seemed to go from strength to strength and in 1861 he was granted a spirit licence. At this time, he was also buying up land and had a number of holdings. It seems that he might have been taking after his father! His largest holding was acquired in 1863 when he purchased the lease of 1,100 acres and 373 acres of freehold land in the Parish of Wallagoot. Another advert appeared in the local newspaper:

> *Manaroo Mercury, 15th April 1864.*
> Merimbula Steam Flour Mills
>
> Having made arrangements for a constant supply of Wheat to arrive direct from Adelaide, the undersigned are in a position to supply flour equal to the Adelaide imported, at Sydney price, with freight only added. All orders forwarded to the undersigned will be faithfully attended to - F Berkelmann or Adam K Page. NB – Bags charged and allowed for when returned.

The business had expanded and there was now a branch in Bega. Later, in February 1865 Adam advertised that owing to ill health he is relinquishing the greater part of his store business and is having a clearance sale. The store was in Bega and run by Anton Sattler who had been the first ferry man in Merimbula. After the closing down sale Anton Sattler, Adam's employee, reopened the store in his own right. Anton eventually became one of the wealthiest businessmen in Bega. Adam tried to run the Merimbula store in a more controlled manner, not extending credit to anyone.

In November 1865 the *Bega Gazette* reported that the inhabitants of Merimbula had determined to erect a place of worship by public subscription. A weatherboard building was proposed at an estimated cost of £40 to £50. A committee of ladies agreed to collect the subscriptions. Martha Page was the Treasurer and Miss

Berkelman the secretary. "The proprietors of the land at Merimbula have given 2.5 acres of land for the site. We report with pleasure that the large landed proprietors of the Bega district have always been most liberal in their gifts when church or school matters are in question. We have no doubt the proprietors of Merimbula will be equally liberal". The report finishes by impressing upon the minds of the people of Merimbula the imperative necessity of a school in connection with the Church:

> *"Now 'tis the spring, and weeds are shallow rooted;*
> *Suffer them now,*
> *and they'll o'ergrow the garden*
> *And choke the herbs for want of husbandry".*

At the end of December, the *Bega Gazette* published a letter from a James Manning of Pambula:

"Sir, I notice in your last issue, that a correspondent of yours makes strictures on my actions, with respect to the giving of land from the Merimbula proprietors to the inhabitants of that locality, for the purpose of erecting a place of public worship.

"I think it necessary to make the annexed remarks on this subject: I offered one of the allotments, that are measured for church reserves, to the Church of England, and to have the deeds made over to the Bishop of Goulburn, in trust. I also offered a similar allotment to the Presbyterians, or to any other religious denomination, the deeds to be made over as may be customary in their churches. But I object to giving over land to nobody and anybody in perpetuity: simply because it is impossible and the meeting of such a question is absurd.

"The proprietors of the land at Merimbula will be ever ready to do what is reasonable and liberal and business-like in such matters: and to which end, under existing circumstances, it strikes me that the only proper way of meeting the present requirements would be to grant a lease, on a peppercorn rent for, say, ten years to Mr Page in trust, for all parties interested in the erection of a suitable school house and place of worship for all denominations, on either of the reserved church allotments; the lease to revert to the proprietors for redisposal by deed of gift, or by a renewal lease, as they may then direct, and as the then altered circumstances of possibly increased population may then induce. In answer to a part of your correspondent's remarks, I may say, that I have a predilection for my own church; but that I have ever shown an intolerant spirit towards the conscientious opinions of any other sect of religion, I deny."

In 1867 Adam and Martha welcomed a visitor to their household. Adam's brother Thompson Scott had sent his oldest son, also Thompson Scott, out to Australia to live with his Uncle and Aunt. The young Thompson was 14, having been born in Adelaide in 1853. This was the age that young men started their apprenticeships. Perhaps, as he had been born in Australia it was deemed a good idea that he could return to the land of his birth and also be an extra pair of hands for Adam with all his business ventures. Martha was now the mother of three children (Emily had died), so she would have been too occupied in looking after them to give very much time to the business. On the 17th December the *Nourmahal*, a Liverpool registered ship of 846 tons arrived in Sydney from London with 24 crew, under the ship's master, John Fowler. There were six cabin passengers, including Thompson Page. Other passengers travelled steerage.

I wonder if young Thompson took the Illawarra ship from Sydney down to Merimbula. I hope he arrived in time for Christmas! However, it wasn't long before the 14-year old was in the sort of scrape that boys of that age seem to always attract. The *Bega Gazette* reported a serious accident on 8th February 1868:

> "We are sorry to hear that a nephew of Mr A K Page met with an accident, which is, we fear, of a very serious nature, involving the amputation of the two middle fingers of the youth's left hand. From such information as has reached us, we learn that Master Page was somewhat incautiously trifling with a pistol charged only with powder. It exploded, and the consequence is that the two fingers are so shattered that Dr Shiels deems amputation necessary."

Oh dear! Not only had Adam and Martha their businesses and children to look after, but an injured nephew as well.

In 1871 Adam was appointed Justice of the Peace (JP), a magistrate, sitting at the Pambula Court House. His appointment was announced in the *New South Wales Police Gazette* on 4th August.

In the *Sydney Morning Herald* of 18th May 1872, there was an announcement that Mrs Adam K Page of Merimbula had been delivered of a daughter on 8th May 1872. This would have been Alice May, who was baptised a month later.

The Pages were taking on staff in the autumn of 1872, according to adverts in the Bega Gazette. Martha wanted "a respectable female as a general servant". Adam wanted "an able willing man to work in the ISN Co's Shipping Stores and to make himself useful. A seafaring man preferred. Wages, six pounds per month and permanent employment for a suitable person."

In December 1873 Adam Kirkaldy Page, together with five other gentlemen was appointed a member of the Public Schools Board for Merimbula by the Governor of New South Wales, via the Colonial Secretary's Office.

With these additional public service offices added to his already large workload it seems that Adam may have not been able to give his businesses full attention. There is intimation that he was struggling financially and soon he decided to sell Penuca Farm, the land and stock. This advertisement for the sale of Adam's Penuca Farm at Jellat Jellat was published on 23 April 1874. A K Page has instructed G Haslingden to sell by public auction on Tuesday 5th May the whole stock of the Penuca Farm, comprising:

> "A K Page's well-known herd of dairy cattle Horses A fine lot of young stock Dairy utensilsFarm implements etc
>
> "The Public are so well aware of the reputation of Mr Page's Cattle, that it is quite unnecessary for the Auctioneer to puff them up."

At the auction Mr R Ritchie purchased the 675-acre Penuca Farm.

On 25th June, the *Bega Gazette* reported the death of A K Page:

Bega Gazette, 25th June 1874

A telegram from Merimbula on Tuesday morning announced the ominous intelligence that Mr A K Page had burst a blood vessel, and that life was in imminent danger. Dr Shiels was at once summoned but, before he could start, a second message brought word that the rupture had proved fatal. Mr Page was one of the early comers to the district. His father was, we are informed, a Major in the British Army*. Nearly 20 years ago Mr Page had employment at Kameruka station, then under the management of Mr James Manning. At Kameruka Mr Page held the position of storekeeper and by his attention to his duties soon gained the manager's confidence; so much so that any business requiring accuracy and despatch always fell to his lot for execution. After some years spent at Kameruka Mr Page opened a store at Merimbula and was afterwards appointed agent to the ISN Company. To residents of this and the Manaro district Mr Page was intimately known and all will regret his death. Gentle and gentlemanly, amiable and upright, kind and courteous, we do not believe he had an enemy in the county. Though of weak constitution, and often much distressed by chronic lung disease, his attention to business – which was onerous, and at times perplexing – was proverbial; and to our knowledge, rather than involve others in trouble, he has frequently paid from his private income compensation for cargo losses that had been caused by neglect or carelessness of others. The ISN Co have lost a servant whose place will not easily be filled. Mr Page married a daughter of the late James Rixon and leaves a widow and five children to an affectionate father. At the time of his decease Mr Page was in his forty first year. Some eighteen months ago he was gazetted a Magistrate of the Colony. The funeral will take place today, leaving Merimbula at 10am and arriving in Bega at 4pm.

And a few days later came the report of his funeral:

Bega Gazette, 2nd July 1874
THE LATE MR PAGE

To the obituary notice given in our last issue we have to add that on Thursday last the funeral procession left Merimbula at 10am and arrived at Bega about 4pm. From Frogs Hollow into Bega a large number of horsemen and conveyances gradually joined the cortege, which contained more than two hundred persons by the time Bega was reached. The remains of the deceased were deposited in the Church of England burial ground in Bega, the service being read by the Reverend A D Faunce.

Adam's grave is in the Bega Cemetery in Anglican section 7, Row E number 7. Poor Martha had lost her husband very prematurely. Although his grave gives his age as 40, I am sure that he was 42, having been baptised in November 1831. Martha was the mother of five young children, ranging in age from 2 to 12. Although the Penuca farm had recently been sold, it might have been to cover debts, rather than being a lump sum that could tide her over for a while.

Martha struggled along in Merimbula for a year, when it was reported in the *Australian Town and Country Journal* on 10th July 1875 that Martha Page, widow and administrator of Adam Kirkaldy Page, deceased, was in the Insolvency Court. The cause of sequestration? Bad debts and other liabilities to the tune of £600 1s 6d. Assets £94 10s. Deficiency, £506 1s 6d. Dire circumstances indeed. What could Martha do? How was she going to survive? Was there anyone who could come to her aid?

*Adam K Page's father, Samuel, was not a major in the British Army. He was a Provision Broker/Merchant in the City of London. He died on 4th June 1860 of a stroke while staying at the Marine Hotel in Hastings, on the south coast of England.

However, Samuel Page's brother-in-law, Lieutenant General Sir William Chalmers (husband of Samuel's half-sister Ann) died in Scotland on 2nd June 1860. Both these deaths would have been announced in the press. Perhaps by the time of Adam's death the two events had become conflated – thus the mention of Adam's father being in the Army.

Chapter 4

Martha Page

Martha's husband Adam had died young, very suddenly, and their five children were still youngsters. In June 1874, when they lost their father, Adelaide was 12, Annie Rose turned nine and William Augustus seven the previous month, Frank was five and Alice just two years old.

Martha's parents, James and Elizabeth Rixon, had originally settled in the Twofold Bay area. James worked for the Imlay brothers before he struck out on his own to enter the shore-based whaling and innkeeping businesses. He secured a licence for the Crown & Anchor, Eden, in 1845 renting it from the Hirst brothers. After they experienced financial difficulties James purchased the property outright in 1848.

Rixon's hotel soon became the venue of choice for all sorts of public activities including meetings, dinners and presentations. For example, in January 1886 Arthur Manning, Commissioner of Crown Lands and Police Magistrates, was guest of honour at a farewell dinner prior to his moving to the Darling Downs & Moreton districts.

James and Elizabeth gained a reputation for their benevolence and in 1858 residents gathered at the Crown & Anchor to present Mrs Rixon with a handsome silver tea service for her "uniform kindness and general philanthropy". The accompanying address noted that "in times of trouble and in the hour of sickness, we have always found you ready to give your assistance".

The Kiandra Gold Rush of late 1859 increased the footfall to the Crown and Anchor and James undertook work to improve the facilities in 1860. However, in 1862 they moved to Bega to take over the Family Hotel, where Adam, Martha and Elizabeth had stayed in 1858. Sadly, James died in September 1863, some nine months before his son-in-law, Adam.

So, both Elizabeth and Martha were widowed within the space of a year. Elizabeth ran the hotel for a year on her own, but then I think she probably moved with Martha. They headed to Sydney where Elizabeth's experience of running a hotel and Martha's need for some financial security saw them taking on 'Strathspey Boarding House' on Macquarie Street, where Martha was the 'chatelaine'.

An advertisement in the *Sydney Morning Herald* of 27th August 1875 reads:

> "The undersigned having purchased the superior BOARD-ING ESTABLISHMENT business, hitherto carried on by Mrs Grant, trusts that she may receive a continuance of the favours accorded to her predecessor, and by strict attention and cleanliness, to merit similar patronage and success.
>
> Martha Page, late of Bega, Sydney 16th August"

Announcements in the Sydney newspapers, prior to Martha taking over, are for births at Strathspey House, so this was a maternity/nursing home. I do not know if it continued in that form under Martha or became a boarding house – which I understand to be a hotel without a liquor licence.

I haven't found too many references to Martha in the newspapers of the time, so I assume that things were running as smoothly as they could be. In 1880 she instructed Rixon & McLeod to sell her former home in Merimbula. The auction was to be held at the Tier's Hotel in Merimbula on 7th July. It was advertised as:

> A commodious dwelling, containing large drawing and dining rooms, 5 bedrooms, coach house, stabling and numerous offices and outbuildings, standing on 5 acres of freehold land.

On 21st June The Postmaster General was sent this letter:

> Sir, I would beg to bring your notice to a sale by auction of a most suitable place for a Post & Telegraph Office at Merimbula. It belonged to A K Page and would if purchased by the foremost repay the outlay as there is no other place available for purchase. I believe it will be bought cheap say from £150 to £200 and as the foremost are now paying over £30 per annum rent, it would well repay them. I do write this as believing that it would be for the interests of the general public the present owner of such property and by so doing have some place to be a surety of their ... and offices.
>
> I enclose you a copy of sureties. If I can be of any service I am at your disposal.
>
> Yours faithfully, Andrew T Gibson

The hammer price was £150 and the purchaser was a Mr Munn. I hope that it didn't go too cheaply. No doubt Andrew T Gibson was disappointed that it was not purchased by the Post and Telegraph company.

On 13th September 1882, Martha's mother, Elizabeth Rixon died in Sydney. Like her son-in-law Adam, she died intestate.

> RIXON – September 23, at the residence of her sister Ann Phibbs, 362 Castlereagh Street, Elizabeth, relict of the late James Rixon, Bega, aged 67 years. Bega papers please copy.

Once again Martha was applying for Letters of Administration. This time it was from the Honourable Courts' Ecclesiastical Jurisdiction. The request was for all the estate, goods, chattels, credits and effects of Elizabeth Rixon to be granted to Martha Page. At this juncture Martha's address was Belmont House, Wynyard Square, Sydney. She had apparently moved on from Strathspey House.

We are all too aware that courts move at a reptilian pace. Sure enough in May 1885, nearly three years later, James Rixon, William Rixon, William Hubbard and his wife Emma (née Rixon) were summoned to the Court in King Street, Sydney to appear personally "to accept or refuse Letters of Administration of the said Estate and Effects of the deceased Elizabeth Rixon; or show cause (if you know any) why the same should not be committed to Martha Page of Balmain, near Sydney, widow, one of the children and next of kin of the said deceased."

In the *Bega Gazette* and *Eden District or Southern Coast Advertiser* of Wednesday 17th June 1885 there was an announcement:

PROBATE – Letters of Administration were granted in the estate of Elizabeth Rixon to Martha Page, a daughter, £500.

In September that year Martha was at the Supreme Court of New South Wales – and was insolvent. Her address is now Vincent Street, Balmain and she is still a boarding house keeper.

On the 2nd September her insolvent estate was placed under sequestration. Martha had to appear for the first and second insolvency meetings on 30th September. The first meeting at 10am was for Creditors to show proof of debts against the estate. The second meeting was fixed for 11am on the same day for further proof and for the election of a Creditors Assignee.

The third meeting was to be held on 13th November 1885. The official Assignee was to give a report, presumably showing the level of debt and whether the Creditors could expect any sort of repayment. The Creditors were also able to state whether Martha would be allowed to keep her household furniture, wearing apparel, beds, bedding, tools of the trade or any part thereof. Poor Martha! The bailiffs were in sight. I do not know what happened. There is no record of the outcome.

None of her children were married at this stage. Their ages ranged from 13 to 24, so the four eldest ought to have been employed, contributing to the family finances, or helping her to run her establishment.

Back in England in June 1860, her father-in-law, Samuel Page had died. After various bequests he left his property and assets to be divided among his seven children. Although he left about £3,000 there were serious liabilities attached to his estate. His children decided not to sell his land in Adelaide, as the value had dropped considerably. They hoped that by holding on to it the value would rise. However, they did share out the land he owned in New Zealand. In September 1860 Adam was apprised of his share, thus:

Department of Lands

The Deeds of Grant specified in this List being ready for delivery to the Grantees, it is requested that early application be made for them at the Office of this Department.

Persons applying for Deeds are particularly requested to state the numbers placed against those they may require.

1533 PAGE Adam K, Auckland, 1 acre 2 roods 18 perches, portion 41

Adam may have sold his acre of prime land in Auckland at the time or Martha may have sold it. Research hasn't turned up any evidence about a sale of the land, so I can only surmise. However, I am sure that Martha remembered that there was land in Adelaide that Samuel Page owned, and which hadn't been sold after he died. Maybe getting Adam's share of his father's land would solve her financial difficulties? However, I expect she would have to get all the Page siblings to agree to the sale.

In 1867, Adam's nephew, Thompson, had come out from England to be an extra pair of hands for her and Adam. Within two months of his arrival he had lost two fingers. Where was he now? He had moved to Hay, Riverina, NSW and had married Clara Margaret Mallagh in Hay in 1880. By 1885, when Martha was having her property sequestrated, Clara had already given birth to three children and one had died.

Martha may have contacted Thompson about the land in Adelaide. She knew that he and his two brothers would have inherited their father's share of their grandfather's property. Thompson could no doubt do with the extra cash now that he was a family man.

After I read Samuel Page's correspondence with Lord Stanley, I spent a considerable time trawling through *Trove*, the Australian newspaper archive, trying to find out more information about Samuel Page.

It was in *Trove* that I came across this announcement:

> *South Australian Register, Monday 24 September 1888*
> Law and Criminal Courts
> SUPREME COURT – IN BANCO
> Tuesday September 25
> T S Page and Others v. Martha Page

This notice was the first I knew of a court case. All the information about Thompson Scott the Elder and Thompson Scott the Younger, as well as Adam and Martha, I gleaned after I had seen this newspaper announcement. For me it was the beginning of a search lasting several years to disentangle all the legal intricacies of the Will of Samuel Page, and it led me to visit the Supreme Court in Adelaide in 2014.

Chapter 5

Court Case 'In Banco'

MARTHA HAD BEEN in straitened financial circumstances. She decided that she should try to get Adam's share of his father's investment in land in Adelaide, South Australia. Surely by now it would have increased in value and might resolve her difficulties?

After Samuel's death in 1860 his seven children decided not to sell the land, it not being worth very much. They thought that if they held on to it the price might rise. Also, it seems that Samuel had borrowed against Trusts that were in his wife's Marriage Settlement. I do not have a copy of the Settlement, but I did find information that indicated that there was some £8,000 that needed 'to be made good' after he died. Had his offspring sold the Adelaide land at that point I believe that the proceeds of the sale would have had to be paid to the Trustees of his Will. It is therefore very understandable that they decided to hold onto the Goodwood Section 8. The Town Acre 335 had been sold in two portions during Samuel's lifetime.

So, in 1888 Martha started legal proceedings to obtain Adam's share, which was now hers, being executrix and beneficiary of his estate. It is difficult, after so many years, to ascertain exactly how she went about this. However, the legal notice in the Sydney paper announced that the case was 'T S Page and others v. Martha Page'.

When I saw this notice for the first time I had no idea who T S Page was. Most of the information in Chapters 3 and 4 was researched after I found the 'In Banco' notification. I was, as I had been for a long time, looking for Samuel Page, in *Trove*. I had seen the correspondence between him and Lord Stanley, so I knew that he had land in Adelaide.

I also knew from the 1841 and 1851 censuses that he lived in South Lambeth. The name of his first child in the census in 1841 was illegible, but looked like Thomasina. That person was not on the 1851 census. Eventually I found out that it wasn't Thomasina but Thompson. Because this is not a common Christian name in England I had guessed at a name that looked similar – such are the pitfalls of research. However, by the time I read the 'In Banco' notice I knew that Thompson Scott Page, born in 1824, had died in 1872. Evidently the T S Page cited in the notice was not him. I subsequently discovered that Thompson Scott Page was in Adelaide in 1851, therefore did not appear in that year's census in the UK.

I had been searching newspaper articles published around 1888, to see whether I could find the outcome of Martha's court case. Nothing came up. I widened my search a few years. Still nothing. Eventually I just put in a general search and got a 'Eureka' moment. The newspaper articles reprinted below came up. Wow! They were dated 1917.

The Advertiser, Adelaide, South Australia, Saturday 7th April 1917

THE PAGE ESTATE

A modern instance near Adelaide of land which has been 'Held in Chancery' and which is now about to be released is afforded by section 8, near the Goodwood railway station, regarding which advertisement appears in another column. This land was purchased by the late Samuel Page, then a provision broker of Catherine Court, Tower Hill, London, in the year 1839, and has been the subject of litigation for the past 30 years. Mr Page's estate at the time of his death, in 1860, was involved in serious liabilities and his children decided that it was not then advisable to sell it.

They therefore entered into various family settlements, which prevented its sale for many years. In 1888 a suit was begun in the South Australian Supreme Court having for its object the sale of the estate. But before it could be settled several of the persons interested in the land died, and the changes finally became so complex that only one of the original ten parties to the suit was living in 1910. In that year Messrs Bakewell, Stow and Piper were instructed to enter fresh proceedings with the object of ascertaining the persons interested in the land and obtaining an order of the court directing it to be sold.

Inevitable legal delays occurred owing to death, marriage, mortgages and assignments while the suit was in progress, but now at length the "dead hand" is about to release its hold and the land is offered for sale. Many incidents of human interest appear in the musty legal documents that comprised the title before the Real Property Act lent its aid.

An entry in the abstract of title, for instance, that Thompson Scott Page, a grandson of the original purchaser was "born on the Sturt in 1853", suggests that at least one of Mr Page's sons visited the distant country in which his father had purchased land, but how long his stay and what his object was are questions that are left unanswered. Again, a judgment of a New Zealand court suggests that Mr Page's activities were worldwide; and an entry of another beneficiary at "Merimbula, Twofold Bay, Australia" suggests that the family had become widely scattered. It only requires a modern novelist to ponder the legal phraseology to bring to life a second Jarndyce vs. Jarndyce but with a happier end, in which some at least of the beneficiaries, after a life-long hope, are rewarded with the increase in value which has taken place during the past 80 years.

The Mail, Adelaide, Saturday 7 April 1917, Real Estate News

PAGE'S ESTATE

Great Suburban Block to be Sold

Romantic History

For many years travellers on the South line have looked at the large section of vacant land near the Goodwood Railway station and have wondered why it has not been cut up for settlement. Rumours have been current that it belonged to the Blue Coat School, or some such institution, and could not be sold. Such rumours are not quite without a foundation, and its history would form the substance for a modern novel on the lines of Bleak House.

The section was originally purchased by Mr Samuel Page, a provision broker, of London on April 1, 1839. Apparently, Mr Page never saw the land, but it seems that one of his sons visited Australia in 1853, because there is an entry in the office of the Registrar of Births, Adelaide, showing the birth of a son at the Sturt on February 5, 1853. Mr Page died in 1860, leaving estate situated in England, Scotland, New Zealand and Australia, but involved in serious liabilities. The beneficiaries under his will were of opinion that conditions in Australia were so gloomy that it would be folly to sell the land, and they decided to settle it upon certain terms until better conditions prevailed. Each of Mr Page's children so dealt with his or her share under the will by means of marriage settlements, assignments, and mortgages that at length it became doubtful who were the persons really interested in the land.

Actions were therefore commenced in the Supreme Court of South Australia and in New Zealand in 1888 to determine the parties interested and to enable the land to be sold but owing to the parties being so widely separated – some in New South Wales, some in England and elsewhere – it became very difficult to proceed, and delays inevitably occurred. Eventually several of the parties died, and by the year 1910 so many changes in interest had occurred that only one of the ten original parties to the action still survived.

Messrs Bakewell, Stow and Piper were therefore instructed to commence fresh proceedings in the Supreme Court of this State to determine the parties interested in the land, including the section at Goodwood, and to obtain a decree of the Court directing the land to be sold. During the present proceedings great difficulty has been experienced owing to the distances between the parties, and to changes of interest, two parties having died during the last two years, but at length finality has been reached, the land has been brought under the provisions of the Real Property Act, and in another column an advertisement appears calling for tenders for the purchase of the section at Goodwood. Messrs Bakewell, Stow and Piper expect shortly to be able to call for tenders for the purchase of certain other lands forming part of the same estate, and thus to bring to a successful conclusion a law suit which has been in progress for 29 years.

The Advertiser, Adelaide, Tuesday 14th August 1917
DIVIDING AN ESTATE

An application was heard by his Honor Mr Justice Buchanan at the Civil Court on Monday, in the case in which Samuel Palgrave Page and others were the plaintiffs, and Henry Stonhewer Freeman and others were the defendants. Charles Wilcox was mentioned as a person who had been served with notice of the judgment, and who had entered an appearance. The matter arose out of a case in which judgment had originally been given in September 1911, and which involved the sale of certain lands at or near Goodwood. The present application was that the cost of all parties should be paid out of the money in court, and that out of the money in courts standing to the credit of the action £22,000 should be paid out and divided by the Master amongst the parties entitled as follows:

Fourteen-eighteenths to the manager of the Executor Trustee and Agency company on behalf of the plaintiffs,

S P Page

R P Page

A S Page

Clara Page

A C Page

Rose Adelaide Blenkarn

one-eighteenth to Charles Wilcox:

and three-eighteenths to such persons as the Master should certify to be entitled thereto as trustees of the share of Mrs Peyton.

Mr A W Piper, KC and Mr W A Norman, appeared for the plaintiff: Mr P F Johnstone for Mrs Rose Phyllis Maude Peyton and for Charles Wilcox: and Mr C H Poxers for all the other defendants. His Honor made an order in the terms of the application.

There was a challenge in the first two articles! A modern-day novelist to record the story, which was akin to Dickens' 'Bleak House' with the Jarndyce vs Jarndyce court case in Chancery. It would have to be a Page descendant. Perhaps it could be me?

However, I was perplexed by the list of recipients of the pay-out of the proceeds from the sale of Section 8 Goodwood. Who were all these people? I knew the Blenkarn surname. Samuel Page's eldest daughter Mary Ann had married Alfred Bower Blenkarn. But I didn't recognise the initials of any of the Pages listed and, as to Charles Wilcox and Mrs Peyton I was completely clueless.

The references to the Adelaide land being worthless at the time of Samuel Page's death led me to search for Samuel's Will, to try and ascertain just who were recipients of his bequests.

Chapter 6

Samuel Page's Will

THE ADELAIDE NEWSPAPER articles reporting the Page Estate settlement in 1917 mentioned that many of the original beneficiaries of Samuel Page's Will had already died. Other than the surnames of some of the lucky recipients of the final judgment having the surname Page I did not know who they all were, or how they were related to Samuel Page.

I started to search for Samuel Page's Will. It was available online, which was lucky, but unfortunately the script was almost indecipherable, being in a style of writing adopted by legal secretaries in that era, before the advent of the typewriter. It took me several days to decipher it, not helped by the legalese used in the Will: words and terms such as 'hereunto', 'hereinafter', 'executors, administrators and assigns', 'give, devise and bequeath'. Since then I have become a little more practised in deciphering legal documents, but this was the first one, and it was difficult.

Samuel's Will was written on 24th November 1855 and the executors were his second son, Samuel Page the Younger, and Benjamin Colaco of Jeffrey's Square, St Mary Axe, a merchant in the City of London. There are some straightforward bequests, mostly of a very modest nature:

He left his sister, Mrs Jane Beech 19 guineas. [A guinea is £1 1s (one pound, one shilling)]. And in case of her dying before his decease the sums of 10 guineas to Ann Beech and Robert Beech, her daughter and son.

Samuel bequeathed his son Samuel £50 and also, after the death of "my dear wife", his gold watch, the two portraits of himself, and portraits of his "dear wife" and his late Uncle, Thompson Scott.

Adam Kirkaldy Page was to receive the miniature portrait of his late Uncle, Adam Kirkaldy. His sister-in-law, Mary Retemeyer was to receive 19 guineas, but if she died before Samuel, then her daughter Jeanette was to receive the same sum. Mary Hawkins, wife of William Hawkins of Hitchin and Elizabeth Henderson, wife of the Reverend William Henderson of Arbroath were both to receive 10 guineas, as a mark of his affection. To Mary Stone-house, mother of his "dear wife" he bequeathed 10 guineas. His employee, John Henry Curwen, if still in his employ at the time of his death, could expect to receive ten guineas.

Then comes something that was absolutely unexpected. It read:

> "I give and bequeath unto my trustees hereinafter named, their heirs and assigns, all that my freehold estate consisting of one acre of land in the projected town of Australind in Western Australia and of one hundred acres of land near the said town, hold the same unto my said Trustees upon trust to pay to my daughter, Mary Ann, the wife of Mr Alfred Bower Blenkarn the rents, dues and profits thereof during the term of her natural life and for her own separate use and benefit, free from and not subject to the debts, control or engagements of the said husband and from and immediately after the decease of my said daughter then I give, devise and bequeath the said several pieces or parcels of land and hereditaments unto all the children of my said daughter living at her decease, their heirs and assigns as tenants in common and not as joint tenants…"

This was an extraordinary piece of information. I had expected to read **Adelaide**. Here was another thread to follow up. Because the text was so difficult to read I could easily have mistakenly read it as Adelaide, but the fact that Western Australia was stipulated

I knew that it could not be Adelaide. So, I was soon to be on the trail of **Australind***.

However, back to the Will! We know from previous chapters that both Thompson Scott Page and Adam Kirkaldy Page had money difficulties and, sure enough, this was alluded to in Samuel's Will:

> "…And do hereby direct that all sums of money owing to me or my firm at the time of my decease from my sons Thompson Scott Page and Adam Kirkaldy Page or from the said Alfred Bower Blenkarn respectively and all sums of money that I may be in any way be liable to pay for in respect of the said Thompson Scott Page, Adam Kirkaldy Page or Alfred Bower Blenkarn respectively shall be debited from and be deducted as part payment of the shares of my estate given unto or intended for the benefit of the said Thompson Scott Page, Adam Kirkaldy Page and my daughter Mary Ann the wife of the said Alfred Bower Blenkarn respectively…"

So, there was no mention of Adelaide at all. No specific mention of any of his land holdings, in Australia and New Zealand, just a generic direction that all his estate should be shared by all his children as tenants in common. This was very frustrating in terms of trying to establish who were the recipients of the sale of Goodwood Section 8 in Adelaide, 57 years after his death.

Even a cursory glance at this Will showed that Samuel Page the Younger, was the 'golden boy'. Thompson had two sons by the time the Will was written, but I do not know what his employment was, or if he had any. Adam was in New South Wales, and not yet married, but seemingly had received money from his father; maybe it was given to him before he sailed to Australia, we shall never know. What we do know is that Samuel Page the Elder was not going to let his sons take advantage. And I guess this was only fair on his other children, Eliza, William and Adelaide, who are not mentioned in the Will. Mary Ann was married in 1848 and by 1855 she had had four of her five children. Her husband, Alfred Bower Blenkarn was a prolific fraudster. There are records of him

51

in the Old Bailey online archive. The Old Bailey was, and still is, the premier criminal court in England. There is more about Mr Blenkarn in a later chapter.

*Australind was so named as an amalgamation of 'Australia' and 'India'. It was proposed initially that horses for the British Army in India would be bred there. It doesn't seem to have taken off to any great extent, but the town does still exist.

Chapter 7

Samuel Page the Younger

IN THE 19TH Century it was common to call sons named after their father, 'the Younger', to distinguish them from 'the Elder'. To avoid any confusion, I will call Samuel the Younger, Samuel Y, to aid my writing and your reading.

Samuel Y was the second son of Samuel and Mary Ann Page, born in 1825, a year after Thompson Scott Page. We know that Thompson Scott spent some time in Adelaide as a young man, married there, had a son and returned to England, where a further two sons were born. There is scant information about Thompson's employment in England and he died fairly young, after being in a nursing home, as he was paralysed.

Samuel Y, meanwhile, had stayed in England and appears to have worked alongside his father as a provision merchant, based initially at 5 Catherine Court, Tower Hill, then at 16 Water Lane, Great Tower Street, both in the City of London. He was evidently conscientious and trustworthy as he was named as an executor in his father's Will. The Will was written in 1855, when Samuel Y was thirty years old, so his father would have been well aware of his capabilities.

I imagine Samuel Page the younger carried out his duties as an executor in an exemplary fashion. One example that came to light was that the land in Australia had been left to Samuel's seven children in equal shares. After Samuel the Elder died in 1860, it was deemed inadvisable to sell the land, as the value had dropped.

However, Samuel Y's sister, Mary Ann, who was married to Alfred B Blenkarn was in financial difficulties. Her six siblings therefore 'bought her out' and she received £671 as one-seventh share of her father's land in Adelaide, which was how it was valued in 1860.

Samuel Y married Mary Anne Palgrave at Marylebone Parish Church on 21st July 1860. The Palgraves were a well-to-do family with property in Bedfordshire and some of her relatives owned a chemist/pharmacy in Bedford. It is rather confusing that both Samuels had 'Mary Annes' for wives. However, Samuel Y's mother had died in 1858 and now his father had also died, so I don't suppose there was any confusion within the family. It is only rather tricky identifying them decades later.

Samuel Y's father had died in Hastings after a stroke at the Marine Hotel. Presumably he had been on holiday. The marriage took place just seven weeks later. Samuel Y no doubt carried on the Samuel Page & Sons business, and was thus able to offer a good, secure, financial position to Mary Anne's father – an assurance that he could keep her in the manner to which she was accustomed. Samuel Y and Mary Anne made their home at Brunswick House, Surbiton in Surrey, where their first son, Samuel Palgrave Page, was born in December 1861. They employed a cook and a general servant. Samuel Palgrave Page was thus a first cousin of my great-grandfather William Augustus Page, born in the same year, but who died in Quetta in 1888.

In due course they moved to St Leonards Lodge on the corner of St Leonards Road and Portsmouth Road in Surbiton. A daughter, Edith Mary was born in January 1864 but she died when only eight months old. Their second son, Robert Palgrave, was born in November 1867. In the 1871 census Samuel Y's occupation is Foreign Produce Broker. His sons are aged nine and three. Mary Anne is not short of help in her home: she now has a nurse, a cook, a housekeeper, a housemaid and a footman. The nurse was Jane Trott, who stayed with the family for many years. With this number of servants, I think one can conclude that this was a family that lived well, entertained on a reasonable scale and enjoyed the good things of life.

In 1873, Elizabeth Garrett Anderson became the first woman to be admitted to the British Medical Association. That year Brunner and Mond joined forces to build the Winnington Works in Northwich, which eventually became ICI (Imperial Chemical Industries) and from which the pharmaceutical company Astra-Zeneca, for whom I worked, was formed. In June 1873 Alice Vickery became the first qualified female pharmacist in the UK.

There was, therefore, much progress in the industrial and medical field. However, all this progress was not to Mary Anne's advantage. Sadly, she died at the young age of 44 in October 1873. Her boys, Samuel and Robert, were aged 11 and almost six respectively. Jane Trott, their nurse, became an important fixture in the lives of the boys, as their father carried on the business (and perhaps immersed himself in work to cope with his bereavement?). Samuel was sent at the usual age of 13 to Bradfield, a public school in Berkshire. In due course Robert attended Harrow, a rather better-known public school.

There didn't seem to be very much information about Samuel Y after this date. However, as is often the case with research, several 'nuggets of gold' happened at once. In Chapters 4 and 5 (about Martha Page) there was mention of the court case against Thompson Scott Page. The case was Number 109 of the South Australia Supreme Court in 1888. It was between Thompson Scott Page, Samuel Page, Eliza Willis (formerly Page), William Augustus Page, Adelaide Page, Willie Parkinson Jay, Edmund Foxcroft Leach, and William Henry Grey who were the Plaintiffs and Martha Page and Samuel Palgrave Page who were the Defendants. This was the application to the court for Martha to obtain Adam Kirkaldy Page's share of his father's lands in Australia. The court case and the outcome are the reason that I became engrossed in writing this book and which I have spent many hours interpreting.

The case forms a later section of the book, but meanwhile it is interesting to explore the nature of the business of 'Samuel Page & Son'.

Samuel Page was a 'foreign produce broker' as stated in the Census, but what did this actually mean? In the New Zealand newspaper, *Otago Witness*, on 16th November 1888 there is a report of a letter received at the Edinburgh office of the New Zealand and Australian Land Company and forwarded to New Zealand by the San Francisco mail. It was from Samuel Page Y, and is a fulsome account of how to export butter and cheese and I will reproduce it in full:

> *NZ Cheese and Butter for the Home Market*
> The New Zealand and Australian Land Co Ltd, Edinburgh,
> 16 Water Lane,
> Tower Street, EC
> London,
> October 3, 1888
> Dear Sirs,
>
> We think it will be well to impress upon shippers of New Zealand cheese and butter the following points, viz:
>
> That all butter of the same mark should be of uniform quality, and that each package of the same mark should be of the same weight and made of the same kind of wood, to ensure regularity of tares, as some wood absorbs more than others.
>
> That if butter be of mottled colour, however good the quality, buyers will only take it at much less money than that which is regular in colour; and colour should be yellow, not red.
>
> That Pond's patent boxes should only be used for butter of exceptionally fine quality, as we understand they cost a good deal more than firkins. The butter in rolls should not be shipped here. That firkins should be bound with galvanised iron hoops, as ordinary iron becomes rusty and looks unsightly.

That stencil plates should always be used to mark the packages, as appearances go a long way, and that the packages should be marked only on the top and that the words "pure butter" must appear on each package.

That there should be no cloth all round butter, but a muslin cloth sprinkled with salt, on the top only.

That butter of fine quality should contain no more than 3 per cent of salt, but anything of doubtful keeping quality may be salted 4 or 5 per cent.

That the London market cannot have quality too good.

That after March it must be expected that prices of New Zealand butter decline very much, because supplies of fresh-made European becomes plentiful.

With reference to cheese, the principal things to bear in mind are that they should be upright Cheddar shape, 50lb to 70lb each in weight, straw coloured, and uniform in colour, not mottled, rich in quality and clean flavoured. There should be a space between the staves of the crates, and a thin board between each cheese, also a scale-board or thin veneer of wood at the top and bottom of each cheese.

We assume that shippers before long will adopt the American mode of packing cheese singly in light boxes instead of several together in a crate, as they are more easily handled.

Having disposed of the bulk of New Zealand cheese and butter from its earliest importation, we have watched with great pleasure the development of the business, and are confident that if shippers continue to improve the quality of their produce very good results will be obtained in this market for the butter from the month of October to March, and there is no reason why the cheese trade should not be carried on all the year round, as the seasons fit in well, as was proved by our being able to dispose of 1800 cases of New Zealand cheese ex Doric and Rimutaka at 50s to 56s, whilst the May and June American offerings at the same time were only worth 46s to 48s.

In conclusion, we strongly recommend that butter be always sent in the refrigerator, and cheese in the cool chamber.

Yours truly (signed)
Samuel Page & Son

This gave me a very good idea of the nature of the business of Samuel Page & Son. It is fascinating to think that the Page company was probably the instigator of importing butter and cheese from the other side of the world, where the seasons were the opposite of those of the 'home country'. Thus, they provided fresh dairy produce for the home market in the winter season, as well as enabling a good living for dairy farmers 'Down Under'.

In 2012 a message popped up on Ancestry.com, but this time it was not from a possible relative. It was from John Eastberg, a historian and the Director of the Pabst Museum in Milwaukee, Wisconsin, USA. And what he told me opened a whole new insight into Samuel Page Y.

John told me that he was writing a history of the Milwaukee Art Museum, which was founded by Frederick Layton in 1888. Frederick Layton had emigrated to the US with his parents when he was a child. The family originated from Great Wilbraham, Cambridge, England. Frederick became a butcher, developing a large meatpacking concern in Milwaukee and eventually started an export business… and who should be one of his business agents in the UK? Yes, it was Samuel Page Y! So, the Samuel Page & Son company was importing dairy produce from New Zealand (and also Australia, as I discovered later) and meat products from the United States. As a foreign produce broker this all seems reasonable and what one would expect, but what John told me next was very unexpected.

At the opening of his art gallery, Frederick Layton gave a speech that was reported in *The Milwaukee Sentinel* on 6th April 1888 and included the following:

"We are largely indebted to Mr Samuel Page of Surbiton near London, an esteemed friend of mine, for the time and interest he has taken in helping me to secure paintings I bought in England. He has also donated to the Gallery a very beautiful painting."

John asked me about Samuel's art collection. This was all news to me. The brother of my great-great-grandfather was a foreign produce broker; I had no idea that he had an interest in art. I couldn't wait to ask John more about this possible connoisseur or collector of art.

John told me that the painting that Samuel had donated to the Milwaukee Art Museum was by William Breakspeare, a Birmingham artist. It was entitled 'The Marriage Settlement' but had been sold out of the collection in 1960. I was distraught! However, John had a photograph that he sent to me, black and white rather than in its original colour, but a lucky find. I confess that I do not like the picture. I find it spooky. I wonder if there is an undercurrent of meaning in the picture. Samuel Page and Mary Ann Stonehouse's marriage settlement of April 1823 was referred to in the South Australian court case and the Trustees of the Settlement were named as defendants in Case 109 in 1888.

Did Samuel Page Y commission this painting for Frederick Layton? Or did he like William Breakspeare's work? I have seen an original by William Breakspeare in Walsall Art Gallery and several of his paintings online; they are mostly of the 'chocolate box' variety. The 'Marriage Settlement' seems quite sinister in comparison. The notes to the painting, displayed at the opening of the gallery, say:

"The Marriage Settlement" by William Breakspeare
"Arranging the Marriage Settlement",

Breakspeare's work, is one of the best figure pieces in the collection. All the things in this picture are selected with rare good taste and painted with consummate skill. The costumes, furniture and tapestries belong to the seventeenth century and unite with the artistic colouring in forming a rich interior. The tall young maiden standing indifferently engaged at her crochet, is well drawn and painted, as are also the seated guardian and attorney, who are arranging the contract for the dowry. The rendering of some legal documents that have fallen upon the floor and a Circassian rug underneath, which time has given an admirable tone, show the educated eye and skilful hand of the artist. It may be predicted that this work will be a favourite with the public.

Frederick Layton had no children and was a philanthropist who gave the people of Milwaukee an art gallery. He wanted to give the public a representative range of the best in contemporary American and European art, but nothing exotic, nor avant-garde Impressionism. The collection reflected his preference for conscientious craftsmanship, and for the beauty of nature in landscapes and human interest in narrative and anecdotal paintings. The 'Arranging the Marriage Settlement' would certainly seem to fit these criteria. Frederick and his wife often travelled to the UK with a niece, and they definitely visited Samuel Page on their visits. His niece recorded these visits in her diary.

Frederick stated in his address at the opening of his gallery that he and his wife had been to Europe at least 20 times. It seems quite amazing to me that folk were careering around the world so much in the days when transport was nothing like as easy as it is in the 21st century. I was also surprised that meat should be coming from Milwaukee, which is about 1,000 miles from New York. Perhaps the meat was shipped through the Great Lakes and out through the St Lawrence Seaway – by 1888 the ships would have had refrigeration.

John also told me that Samuel Page had been present for the opening of the gallery and that his signature was in a club guest book. This was fascinating, as I have few original documents on the Pages. Most information has come via the Internet or newspapers.

After John had talked about Samuel Page having an art collection, I was rather sceptical of the idea. And how, in any case would I find out? My feeling was that Samuel would have, like many of us, bought paintings that he liked and hung them in his house;

not necessarily in a 'gallery' within the house, though of course that was a possibility. I like to think that he enjoyed looking at the art that he bought and had hung it in various rooms around his house. I researched the house and discovered that after Samuel died the house was occupied by Dr Thomas Barnardo and his family, and later by a Herbert Hill, who was a lawyer. The house had 15 rooms, so there was plenty of space for artwork.

The art interest of Samuel Page Y had sparked my curiosity, so my next move was to obtain a copy of his Will. One thing of which I am sure is that families either have money or children: to have both is a luxury. Thompson Scott had three sons, but was paralysed, so seems to have left nothing – certainly no Will exists. Adam Kirkaldy also died intestate, leaving several children and some debt. However, Samuel Y had married well, had only two sons and built up the business that his father had founded. He died on 26th December 1890, aged 64. When I located his Will I discovered that he had left £47,668 6s 9d. This was a substantial sum, equivalent to £4.25 million in 2018.

Being interested in art myself, I felt an affinity to Samuel and when I read his Will I rather liked him. He didn't seem quite as mercenary as his father. He gave his sister Adelaide £2,000 because she had been kind to all her relatives. He also gave Martha Page £100 and cancelled the £200 debt that Adam had owed him, and he asked his Trustees to deliver up to Martha all securities for the debt. His old nurse, Jane Trott, who had been in the family's service for many years received 50 guineas. There are other specific bequests but near to the end of the Will is the proof of his artistic sensibilities, bequeathing all jewellery, china, linen, musical instruments, wines etc. to his two sons. He then states:

> "And as to the pictures and water colour drawings, I desire
> that each son shall choose one picture or drawing – my elder
> son to have the first choice and so on until all have been
> chosen."

It seems, therefore, that he did have quite a collection of art but there is no indication of how many paintings and drawings he owned. It would have been wonderful to have known or seen some of these pictures and indeed they did pass down the family, as described in later chapters. The family portraits that Samuel Y inherited from his father were passed down to his son, Samuel Palgrave Page.

And of course, Samuel Y's one-sixth share of his father's estates in Australia would now pass to his sons. Samuel Palgrave Page and Robert Palgrave Page would each have a one-twelfth share. Samuel and Robert were now very wealthy men, and their stories will be expanded in later chapters.

As a footnote, the Layton Art Museum, which was based on the design of the Walker Art Gallery in Liverpool in the UK, no longer exists. There is now a fabulous modern art gallery which can be viewed online.

William Augustus Page 1888-1946, Squadron Quarter Master Sergeant, King Edward's Horse.

Sent to his fiancée, Florence Emily Spencer. "Rather poor but I think you will see it is me".

William Augustus Page 1888-1946.

Squadron Quarter Master Sergeant, King Edward's Horse, on his horse. "Not very good but no doubt answers the purpose". Sent to Florence Emily Spencer.

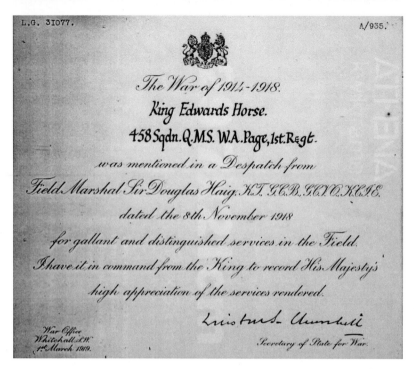

William Augustus Page, 'Mentioned in Dispatches' on 8th November 1918 for "gallant and distinguished services in the field". Signed by Winston Churchill.

St Paul's pro-Cathedral, Valletta, Malta, where William Augustus Page, 1861-1888, and Mary Ann Briggs were married in November 1885.
Queen Adelaide laid the foundation stone in March 1839.

Edith Frances Elizabeth Page, born 23rd August 1886. Photographed at her baptism by Formosa Guiseppe Lorenzo, Strada Forni, Valletta.

Quetta Cantonment, Baluchistan, India, c.1890.

Christmas at Quetta, c 1890.

Robert Denny Briggs, the grandfather
who brought William Augustus Page
back to England.

Harry Robert Briggs, 'Uncle Harry' to
William Augustus Page.
Photo c.1910.

Centre of Adelaide diagram from 1839 showing town acres.

A cathedral was proposed to be built between Town Acres 335 (Samuel Page's) and 338, but the project was not realised.

Victoria Square is also known by the aboriginal name Tarndanyangga.

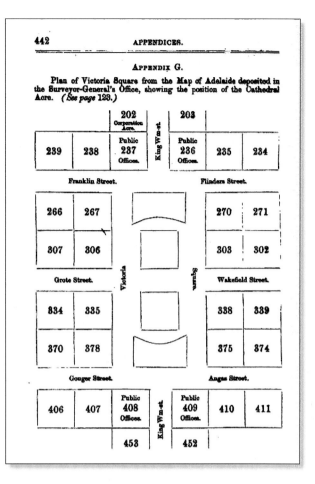

APPENDIX G.

Plan of Victoria Square from the Map of Adelaide deposited in the Surveyor-General's Office, showing the position of the Cathedral Acre. *(See page 123.)*

Reed Beds Adelaide, which Thompson Scott Page gave as his address on his marriage to Helen Best in 1851.

'The Marriage Settlement' by William Breakspeare (1856-1914).
Donated by Samuel Page to the Layton Art Gallery, Milwaukee, in 1888.

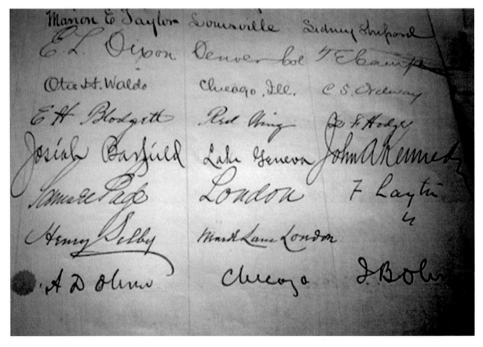

Signature of Samuel Page at F Layton's Club.
Opening of Layton Art Gallery, Milwaukee, 1888.

Chamber of London, *11ᵗʰ* Day of *May* 18*5 9*
Born *Without* the Liberty of the City, to
wit at *the Parish of St Mark
Kennington Surrey* —

William Augustus Page

Son of *Samuel Page*
Citizen and Goldsmith of London, came before the Chamberlain,
the day and year aforesaid, and desired to be admitted into the
Freedom of this City by Patrimony, in the said Company of Goldsmiths, because he is legitimate and was born after the admission of
his Father into the said Freedom   The admission of his Father is
entered in the Book marked with the Letter *C* and bears date
the *13ᵗʰ* day of *January* in the *58ᵗʰ* Year of
the Reign of *George 3ᵈ*

and in the Year of our Lord *1818*

*Copy 1818
Born 1836*

Presented by *Henry John Lias* Warden.

W E declare, upon the Oaths or Declarations we severally took at the
time of our Admission into the Freedom of this City, that
William Augustus Page is the Son of *Samuel Page*
Citizen and Goldsmith of *London*, and that he was born in lawful Wedlock,
after the Admission of his Father into the Freedom of this City;
and that he is his Son so reputed and taken to be, and so we all say.

William Nash

W B Drury Jun

1938/33/A

Freeman of the City of London, granted by patrimony to
William Augustus Page, 1836-1896.

Martha Page's grave, Manly, New South Wales, Australia.

Chapter 8

Mary Anne Page

MARY ANNE WAS the third child and first daughter of Samuel and Mary Ann Page, baptised at St Mark's Church, Kennington on 26th September 1827. As with all the Page children of that generation there is little known about them, apart from appearing in the census records (which began in England in 1841), until they were married.

Mary Anne married Alfred Bower Blenkarn at St Michael's Church Stockwell on 23rd May 1848. She was 20 years old. This was three years after her father's fruitless correspondence with the Lord Stanley. It is very likely that Samuel's finances were strained, as he was getting no return from his Australian investments. At this distance in time it is impossible to know whether this was a love match or a pragmatic solution. Prior to the 1882 Married Women's Property Act, English law defined the role of the wife as a 'feme covert'. This emphasised her subordination to her husband, putting her under the 'protection and influence of her husband, her baron or lord'.

Samuel may well have been pleased to marry Mary Anne off. She would be one less offspring to support and would be her husband's responsibility. There was a Marriage Settlement for Mary Anne but it is not a public document and I do not know the contents. These settlements were quite often put in place by fathers to ensure that their daughter had some small income, known as 'pin money', of her own. I still wonder whether Samuel Page Y was influenced by events that he had witnessed during Mary Anne and Alfred's marriage when donating 'The Marriage Settlement' painting to Milwaukee Art Museum.

Mary Anne's beau, Alfred, lived at St Ive's Cottage on St Anne's Road in Lambeth. Mary Anne was living in her father's house at 2 Lansdowne Road, also in Lambeth. They might have met at church or even promenading at the Vauxhall Pleasure Gardens. Surrey County Cricket ground, the Oval at Kennington, was very nearby and was licensed as a cricket ground in 1845, although the first recorded match, London versus Dartford took place 120 years previously.

Hopefully it was a nice sunny day as they started out on married life. Alfred was an architect, so Samuel would hope that Mary Anne could look forward to a decent standard of living and a bright future. Alfred's father, John Blenkarn, was a wharfinger, an owner or keeper of a wharf. He took responsibility of goods delivered to the wharf, probably had an office on the wharf or dock and took care of day-to-day activities including slipways, keeping tide-tables and resolving disputes. The term wharfinger is now obsolete. The modern equivalent would be dockmaster.

There were two other family events in 1848, one of sorrow, one of joy. Samuel Page's half-sister Ann, who was brought up by Aunt Jane and Uncle Adam in Arbroath, married Lieutenant General William Chalmers of the 52nd Regiment, who had fought in the Peninsular Wars and at Waterloo with Wellington. They resided in Dundee and also on their country estate, Glenericht, near Blairgowrie and Rattray. In 1846 Queen Victoria knighted William Chalmers. Samuel's sister therefore became Lady Ann Chalmers.

In 1845 their eldest son, also William, a Lieutenant in the 11th Regiment sailed from Greenwich to Van Diemen's land, now known as Tasmania. At the young age of 18, he was the second in command of the military escort taking 298 convict prisoners to their punishment 'over the seas'. He was in the southern hemisphere for three years. On the return voyage to England in 1848, he sadly died at sea. The announcement of his death and Mary Anne's marriage appear alongside each other in some newspapers.

Just nine months after their marriage, in January 1849, Mary Anne and Alfred's first child was born, a daughter named Marianne.

Mary Anne Blenkarn (née Page) had a cousin, Mary Voute (née Retemeyer). Mary Anne and Mary were the daughters of the twin sisters Mary Anne and Mary (née Stonehouse). There was a surfeit of Mary's and Mary Anne's! Mary Retemeyer was a similar age to her cousin, Mary Ann Page. They were both married in 1848 and Mary Retemeyer, now Voute, also gave birth to a baby girl in 1849... and she called her Mary! The twins must have been delighted to both become first-time grandmothers in the same year, and to have granddaughters named after themselves.

In 1851 Mary Anne and Alfred were living at St Ives Cottage, St Anne's Road in Lambeth. Alfred's occupation was architect. Marianne was two years old and she had a baby brother, Alfred Elstone Blenkarn, who was nine months old. There were also servants in the household: Mary Johns and Mary Linkes were house servants, and James Williams was the groom. Samuel Page would have been pleased to see this young family doing so well and prospering. Two more children arrived in the next couple of years. Another girl, Alice, was born on 8th April 1852 and William Chalmers in 1853. This little boy was evidently named after Mary Anne's eminent Scottish uncle, Sir William Chalmers.

Mary Anne now had four children under the age of five. Pressure would be on their finances, but perhaps Mary Anne did not know just how much pressure. Did Alfred share his concerns with her? Perhaps he tried to rectify the situation by reckless methods. I began to find bankruptcy notices in the *London Gazette* from 1855. Thompson Scott Page was back in England from Australia. I wonder if he was an influence on Alfred? Certainly, Thompson Scott had been bankrupted in Adelaide.

The *London Gazette* of 14 September 1855 has the following piece:

Court for Relief of Insolvent Debtors

The following PRISONER, whose Estates and Effects have been vested in the Provisional Assignee by Order of the Court for Relief of Insolvent Debtors and whose Petitions and Schedules, duly filed, have been severally referred and transmitted to the Country Courts hereinafter mentioned, pursuant to the Statute in that behalf, are ordered to be brought up before the Judges of the said Courts respectively, as herein set forth, to be dealt with according to the Law:

Before the Judge of the County Court of Suffolk, holden at the Shirehall in Ipswich on the 14th day of September 1855 at Nine o'Clock in the Forenoon precisely.

Alfred Bower Blenkarn (sued as Alfred B Blenkarn) formerly of Courland, Wandsworth Road, Wandsworth, Surrey, Architect and Surveyor, then of Gravesend, Kent out of business, then of Boulogne sur Mer, in the Kingdom of France, then of Jewin Street, Aldersgate Street in the City of London, out of business, then of 125 St John's Street, Islington, out of business, then of Kew Green occupying apartments there, then of Pagoda Cottage, Kew Road, then of 2 Castle Terrace, Hill Street, then of Richmond Green both in Richmond – all in Surrey. And whilst residing at the four last-named places having offices at 3 Sise Lane, Bucklesbury, City of London Architect & Surveyor, then lodging at the Swan Inn, Stratford, Essex, then of 5 Tenterden Street, Hanover Square, Middlesex and then and late of 3 Park Terrace Fonnereau Road, Ipswich, Suffolk, occupying apartments there, out of business."

Good gracious me! Alfred certainly got around. Was he doing a series of 'moonlight flits'? There is no indication of the timescale. Had this been going on since their marriage in 1849? He was listed as residing at St Ives Cottage in April 1851. It looks as if he's been trying to escape the situation by heading off to Essex and Kent then going across the Channel to France. There isn't any indication of the reason for the Bankruptcy, nor of the sentence. However, he was evidently already being held in the Debtors Prison in Ipswich.

Just over a year later, 4th November 1856 there is another listing in the *London Gazette*.

> "Alfred Bower Blenkarn, formerly a Prisoner of Debt in the County Gaol of Ipswich, Suffolk, then of 3 Lacey Terrace, Penton Place, Newington, Surrey next and late of Veranda Cottage, Blackheath Hill, Greenwich, Kent. Architect and Surveyor, having an office first at 90 Cannon Street West and then at 11 Coleman Street, both in London, at which said offices he also described himself as Auctioneer and Land Agent, but did not take out an Auctioneer's licence, or ever act as Auctioneer."

Some light is now thrown onto the situation. Although Alfred has given his profession as Architect on his marriage certificate and in the census, he also described himself as an auctioneer for which he never took out a licence. Or was the whole thing a charade? If he wasn't an Auctioneer as stated in the Gazette paragraph, had he ever been an Architect? This must have been very difficult time for Mary Anne. She had four children to care for, and her husband was in Debtor's Prison. Her father would also have been distressed, as he'd hoped that Alfred would look after his daughter.

Perhaps Samuel the Elder and his son Samuel came to Mary Anne's rescue. There aren't any more items in the *London Gazette* about Alfred Blenkarn until 1862. Mary Anne's mother, Mary Anne the Elder died on 19th February 1858. Alfred must have been around for some of the time during 1857, because a third daughter, their fifth child, Rose Adelaide, was born the day after Mary Anne the Elder died. Samuel the Elder died in June 1860; his estate had 'serious liabilities'. Could this have been caused because he'd been bailing out Alfred and Mary Anne? We know that the family did not want to sell his lands in Adelaide and elsewhere, but they put together a 'rescue package' for Mary Ann, so she did have £600+ given to her.

In the 1861 census Alfred and Mary Anne are back in Lambeth at 11 Winterslow Place, Brixton. Alfred is now 34 and Mary Anne a year younger. Marianne is 12 and Alice eight. William Chalmers is seven and Rose Adelaide is three. Rose was named after Aunt Adelaide, Mary Anne's youngest sister, who was living with them, now that both her parents were deceased. Despite the several bankruptcies they still have a couple of servants. Maria Martin is the cook and Sophie Shepherd is their general servant. Alfred Elstone is 11 years old and at school on the other side of the River Thames; Aske's Hospital School at Shoreditch/Hoxton. This eventually became the renowned Haberdasher's Aske's School.

Adelaide is listed as being of 'Independent Means'. Single women were legally 'feme sole' and could control their own money and property, not being subjugated by a husband. However, the 'happy home' wasn't going to last very long.

On page 9 of *The Times* on the 18th November 1862 there was a report, as follows:

A B Blenkarn

The bankrupt has been an architect. This was his fourth failure. Since this bankruptcy he has again become bankrupt. Having been taken in execution in June last, the Commissioner decided that his release could not be ordered until this (the fourth) bankruptcy had been disposed of. The bankrupt now applied for a certificate accordingly, supported by Mr Reed. Mr Burton appeared for the assignees. The leading features of the case have been already reported in *The Times*

It was now mentioned that, having been three times insolvent, and being in a deficiency of £370, the bankrupt in one year purchased goods on credit to an amount exceeding £50,000, obtained cash advances to the extent of two-thirds of the invoiced prices from the Mercantile Bank of India and other banking houses, and consigned the goods to parties at Bombay and elsewhere. The result was a loss of £22,000 to the creditors, less a dividend of about 5d in the pound.

The COMMISSIONER said it was astonishing that a man of the bankrupt's antecedents could have thus obtained credit*. The bankrupt had acted most fraudulently.

For the bankrupt it was urged that the creditors knew what he was about to do with their goods, and they did not complain.

His HONOUR – My present opinion is that I cannot grant the bankrupt a certificate. I will consider the matter and give my judgement on Monday next.

(The case was conducted before Mr Commissioner HOL-ROYD)

*[£50,000 in 1862 would be worth approx. £4.4 million in 2017. No wonder the Commissioner was astonished!]

Four months later, the *London Gazette* of 17th February 1863 has a listing of Alfred Bower Blenkarn, operating business at an even longer list of addresses than in 1856. He was "adjudicated bankrupt on the 12th February and was carrying on a business at 81 Mark Lane as a Commission Agent. He is required to surrender himself to Thomas Ewing Winslow a Registrar of Her Majesty's Court of Bankruptcy on the 5th March at 1 o'clock precisely. Mr George Coleman of 25 Coleman Street is the Official Assignee and Messrs Wood and France of Aldersgate Street are the Solicitors acting in the bankruptcy."

On August 7th, 1863, The *London Gazette* records that Alfred Blenkarn who having recently been in the London and Middlesex Debtors Prison was discharged from Bankruptcy on 29th June. Every couple of years Alfred Blenkarn is up before the Bankruptcy Court. He mostly seems to talk his way out of the situation, by paying off a small amount of the bankruptcy, based on future earnings. However, quite often the future earnings are fraudulent.

One of his frauds, tried at the Old Bailey, is featured as an example of 'fraud on the seller by impersonation' in the book entitled 'The Law of Contracts' by Samuel Williston. The details of the case are quite heavy going but illustrate the lengths to which Alfred Blenkarn went in his fraudulent dealings.

It took place in 1878. The case 'Cundy v. Lindsay' was a dispute about title to goods and it reached the House of Lords. A rogue called Blenkarn had a room at 37 Wood Street, Cheapside. A well-known firm called W Blenkiron & Son carried on business at 123 Wood Street. Blenkarn placed written orders for goods from 37 Wood Street, with the plaintiffs. He signed the orders in such a way that the signature appeared to be Blenkiron & Co. The plaintiffs who knew of Blenkiron and Son, though not the number at which they carried on business in Wood Street, accepted the orders and despatched goods addressed to 'Messrs Blenkiron & Co, 37 Wood Street'. Blenkarn sold some of these goods to the defendants, against whom the plaintiffs claimed in conversion.

The House held that no contract had been concluded with Blenkarn and that, accordingly the property in the goods had remained vested in the plaintiffs. Lord Cairns remarked that the plaintiffs and Blenkarn never came into contact personally and that everything that was done was done by writing. The problem was the conclusion to be derived from the writing, as applied to the facts of the case. He held that Blenkarn had deliberately led the plaintiffs to believe that they were contracting with Blenkiron & Co, an existing firm. He asked:

> "…how is it possible to imagine that in that state of things any contracts could have arisen between the Respondents and Blenkarn, the dishonest man? Of him they knew nothing and of him they never thought. With him they never intended to deal. Their minds never even for an instant of time, rested upon him, and as between him and them there was no consensus of mind which could lead to any agreement or any contract whatever."

Lord Hatherley said, [at p 469]:

> "… from beginning to end the Respondents believed that they were dealing with Blenkiron & Co. They made out their invoices to Blenkiron & Co, they supposed they sold

to Blenkiron & Co, they never sold in any way to Alfred Blenkarn; and therefore Alfred Blenkarn cannot by so obtaining the goods, have by possibility made a good title to a purchaser as against the owners of the goods, who have never in any shape or way parted with the property nor with anything more than the possession of it."

Lord Penzance said [p 471]:

"In the present case Alfred Blenkarn pretended that he was, and acted as if he was, Blenkiron & Co with whom alone the vendors meant to deal. No contract was ever intended with him, and the contact which was intended failed for want of another party to it."

Here, once again, the focus was on the intention of the offeree. In deciding that his intention was to contract with Blenkiron & Co, the House had regard to the fact that the order was apparently signed 'Blenkiron' & Co' and to the fact that the plaintiffs knew of a firm of that name and intended to deal with that firm. Thus, extrinsic evidence was admitted in addition to the wording of the order in order to ascertain the intention of the plaintiffs. He was found guilty.

On 24th September 1879, Mary Anne died in Shepherds Bush, aged 52. She'd been suffering from bronchitis for some time but died after a twelve-hour bout of pulmonary congestion. She was buried at West Norwood Cemetery, South London.

I feel that I haven't given Mary Anne a voice, but she lived in an age where many married women were considered 'goods and chattels'. I have no way of knowing the quality of her life, whether she wished she was rid of Alfred or whether she loved him dearly, despite all the shame and difficulties he had heaped upon her. Or was he just a loveable, inept rogue?

Alfred carried on in various guises. From being an architect and general merchant, he listed himself as a paper merchant in 1881 and was living with his youngest daughter, Rose, on Darville Road in Hackney. In the Central Criminal Court Session of 27th March 1882 Alfred Bower Blenkarn was up before the Law again, for 'obtaining goods by false pretences'. He was handed five years of penal servitude. In the 1891 census he's living in Jersey in the Channel Islands. He is a Commission Agent, lodging with a widow and her daughter!

He died in 1901, aged 74 and is buried at Abney Park cemetery in London.

Chapter 9

Eliza Page

AFTER HER FATHER died in 1860 Eliza, his second daughter, went to live with her younger brother, William Augustus and his wife Frances in Godalming. Augustus and Frances had one young son, born in 1860 and another on the way. Eliza, as a capable 31-year-old, would be a help to her younger sister-in-law. In the Victorian era woman of her age would probably be considered 'on the shelf'. Eliza did have some opportunities to meet suitable young men. For example, in the fifties, she had been to stay with her Retemeyer cousins in Oxton near Birkenhead. There were several sisters, children of her mother's twin sister Mary and her naturalised British husband Mynhard Retemeyer, born in The Netherlands. There is no doubt she joined with them and their brothers in socialising. It was unfortunate for Eliza that her father's estate was left with serious financial liabilities. This would definitely have affected her marriage prospects.

Somehow or other she did manage to find a husband but it's doubtful whether he was a good catch financially. His name was George Goodwin Willis and they were married on 2nd November 1861, by which time Eliza was 32. The ceremony took place at Surbiton District Parish Church and it seems that her elder brother Samuel hosted the event. He of course lived in Surbiton and had himself been married the year previously. He was a witness to Eliza's marriage and the other witness was George's uncle, Ralph Willis, a farmer of Burnham Abbey, Bedfordshire. They settled in

St Johns Wood and her younger sister Adelaide lived with them for some period. George was a wholesale stationer. He had been declared bankrupt in the 1850s. Bankruptcy seems to have run in the family, except for the 'Samuel Pages'. Looking at the bankruptcy listings in that era it was a not uncommon occurrence, there are dozens listed every day.

In the 1871 census Eliza is living at St John's Wood, north London, and her younger sister Adelaide is living with her, together with a domestic servant and a lodger. But George isn't listed. Where could he be?

What I discovered was rather shocking and redolent of his brother-in-law, Alfred Bower Blenkarn.

The *London City Press* reported in December 1870:

> *Charge of Embezzlement*
>
> George Goodwin Willis, 40, traveller, was brought up on remand, charged with embezzlement whilst in the service of Mr Harris, wholesale stationer. The circumstances of the case have already been reported. The prosecutor now expressed his willingness to withdraw the charge. The prisoner had expressed the utmost penitence for his conduct, which for years had been the source of great anxiety for him. His family who were highly respectable, had been plunged into the deepest distress at the position in which he was placed, and had arranged that he should go abroad if his lordship consented to the course that had been proposed. The Lord Mayor acceded to the application and discharged the prisoner.

The case was also reported in *The Globe*:

> Police Courts – MANSION HOUSE – In the case of George Goodwin Willis, a commercial traveller, who had been charged with an embezzlement of upwards of £400 belonging to Mr Harris, a wholesale stationer in Pancras Lane, it was stated yesterday that the prosecutor had withdrawn the complaint on receiving an explanation from the accused, and in consideration of the good character he had borne for some years. The Lord Mayor, after ascertaining that there

had been no compromise in the matter, discharged the prisoner. Mr Fox solicitor for the prosecution; Mr St John Wontner for the defence.

As George isn't listed in the 1871 census it would seem a fair bet that he did go abroad for some time. In 1881 he and Eliza and a general servant were living in the Pancras parish of St Peters. He gives his occupation as wholesale stationer. George didn't make the 1891 census. His death announcement, in a Wrexham newspaper that year, reads:

WILLIS – March 12th, aged 58 years, at 53 Doughty Street, London WC, after a long and painful suffering, George Goodwin Willis.

His Will is rather interesting. Thinking back to previous chapters we remember that Samuel Page the Elder had a half-sister, Elizabeth, who was raised by her Aunt Jane and Uncle Adam in Arbroath and who then married the Rev William Henderson of St Mary's Episcopal Church, Arbroath. Two of Elizabeth's sons are named as executors of George's Will: Rev Charles Greenhill Henderson Hamilton, laird of Dalserf, Nether-burn, and William Duncan Henderson of Old Broad Street, City of London.

His Will was written in 1889. George made bequests of £200 each to Mary Ann Blenkarn's daughters, Marianne, Alice and Rose. £400 was bequeathed to Elizabeth Henderson, the daughter of William and Elizabeth Henderson and sister of his executors. Elizabeth was to inherit the remainder of his estate if his wife, Eliza, predeceased him.

Eliza did not die until 1906, and thus did not predecease him. However, she did not seek probate for his Will. Probate was not granted until after Eliza's death. His executors renounced Probate and so it was Alice Platt (née Blenkarn), Mary Ann's middle daughter, who obtained Probate. The value was £951.

Prior to her death, Eliza continued to live in Doughty Street, off Russell Square, London. These days the Charles Dickens Museum is situated on the street, as well as Doughty Street Chambers, home of the human rights practice of Geoffrey Robertson QC. Amal Clooney is one of his most eminent barristers, specialising in human rights and international law.

After George died, Eliza moved along the street to number 50. By the time of the 1901 census all her siblings had pre-deceased her. The property is listed as a private house and was divided into three apartments. Eliza, now aged 71, had a young general servant named Flora Baker living with her.

Residing further along the street was a solicitor called Charles Edward Newnham. His practice was at 19 East Cheap in the City of London. Charles was a widower and had three young children, Rose, Agnes and Horace. Eliza must have taken a liking to these children, as she and George had no children of their own.

Eliza's Will reflects her personality and what one imagines to be a rather Victorian décor and house style. She was very generous in her bequests to Rose Phyllis Maude Newnham, daughter of Charles Newnham, leaving her a diamond half-hoop ring, a signet ring, her eiderdown, folding bedroom table, all books and music, four chairs and two stools from the sitting room and all pictures and photographs labelled with her name. Also, her silver watch and Shepherd's Plaid shawl, the linen cupboard on the second landing with the linen inside, the piano which had belonged to her sister Adelaide, her travelling holdall for rugs and silver bangle, engraved 'Bobby' inside.

I wonder what Rose's reaction was. She was about 15 or 16 at the time. Did she think it would form the basis for her own household when she was older, or did she think 'what a lot of old junk'?

There were small bequests to Eliza's nephews Samuel Palgrave Page, Robert Palgrave Page and Alfred Samuel Page. These three men were all very well off. She left nothing to her six nieces and nephews, the children of her brother William Augustus. Her instructions to her executors about giving away her apparel were very specific: nothing to be given to her nieces Alice Platt, Rose Blenkarn and Marianne Taylor, the daughters of her sister Mary Anne!

The minutiae are rather amazing. Her ebony walking stick and gold spectacles were to go to Dr J Rees Gabe. Mrs Larder of Whitechapel was to receive her invalid bed. She also asks that debts incurred by her husband, if not settled in her lifetime, be paid to Dr Harry Scott of Southdown House Eastbourne, and Mr Wilson, chemist of 80 Lambs Conduit Street.

Her cousin, Helena Retemeyer, of Colwyn Bay received a tapestry that had been worked by their mothers, Mary Ann Page and Mary Retemeyer (twins, née Stonehouse). Also, a photograph of her mother and a painting of Grandfather and Grandmother Stonehouse. Then comes a rather sad paragraph:

> "Whereas by an Indenture of Settlement dated the 31st day of October 1861 made in contemplation of my marriage with my late husband George Goodwin Willis certain monies and premises were settled upon Trusts for the benefit of myself and my husband for life, and subject thereto upon trust on failure of children of our marriage for such person and in such manner as I should by Will appoint.
>
> And whereas my said Husband is deceased and there has been no issue of my said Marriage…
>
> ….to hold the said Trust property in Trust for the said Rose Phyllis Maude Newnham absolutely."

Well, Rose Phyllis Maude Newnham did very well from this elderly, childless lady. But oh, how her inheritance caused delays and difficulties with the division of Samuel Page's land in Adelaide! We'll meet RPM Newnham in a later chapter. Meanwhile we move onto Eliza's younger siblings, Adam Kirkaldy, James Stonehouse, William Augustus and Adelaide.

Adam has already had a chapter devoted to him. James was born in 1833 and named after his maternal grandfather. Eliza was four and Adam two when James was born. Sadly, James had a very short life and died in January 1839 when he was five years old. There would have been great sorrow at Culloden House. Although infant mortality was high in the Victorian era, the loss of a child would have cast a shadow over the whole household. Mary Ann must have had her hands full, nursing a sick five-year old, as well as looking after William Augustus, almost three and Adelaide just one-year old.

One wonders what effect James Stonehouse's death had on his siblings. I haven't been able to find any records of whether he was buried at West Norwood cemetery, which seems to be where other deceased family members were interred.

Chapter 10

William Augustus Page

AT LAST I have arrived at my direct ancestor, William Augustus Page. Born 1836, he was my great-great-grandfather. His son, William Augustus Page, died in India in 1888 and his grandson, also William Augustus Page, my grandfather, was born in India in 1888.

I had imagined that perhaps the name Augustus was used because the child was born in August, but he wasn't. The name of Samuel Page's home, 'Culloden House' gave me the answer. The Battle of Culloden was the final confrontation of the Jacobite uprising of 1745. In April 1746 the Jacobite forces of Charles Edward Stuart were trounced by Hanoverian forces commanded by William Augustus, Duke of Cumberland. This conflict was the last pitched battle fought on British soil. I have no idea at all why Samuel Page would name his child and house after Culloden. Answers on a postcard please!

I discovered that Samuel Page had *three* grandsons named William Augustus: Adam Kirkaldy Page's first son was named William Augustus as was Thompson Scott Page's third son.

William Augustus (the first) was the youngest, and fifth, son of Samuel and Mary Ann Page. He was three years old when his older brother James Stonehouse died. He was only nine when his father corresponded with Lord Stanley suggesting the Government's dereliction of duty with regards to his land in Adelaide, so it was likely to have had less impact on him than on his three older brothers. His playmate was probably his sister Adelaide, two years his junior.

By the time he was 22 he was living in Queens Road Villas, Kentish Town. He was now north of the River Thames, having lived most of his life in South Lambeth. While in Kentish Town he met Frances Hussey, his future wife. Frances was born in Bow, East London. Her parents, Thomas and Elizabeth were both deceased. Elizabeth had died in 1852 when Frances was only 12 years old. Her father, Thomas, married his second wife, Esther Lane, in 1857 but died in 1858. On his wedding certificate he is listed as commission merchant, but the Probate records him as Landlord of the Hop Pole pub. There is an unusual additional entry in the cemetery record – his coffin was 2ft wide.

Frances was the youngest of the five daughters of Thomas and Elizabeth. When she married William Augustus Page her address is also given as 12 Queens Road Villas, Kentish Town. William and Frances were married by Special Licence, which William applied for on 15th November 1858. I am wondering if he was known as William or Augustus. His signature on the Special Licence request is Wm Augustus, which indicates that he used the name Augustus. However, it is impossible to know for sure. After the usual statements about believing that there is no impediment to the marriage there is a handwritten postscript, "and he lastly made Oath that the said Minor hath no father living, or Testamentary Guardian of the person lawfully appointed, or Mother living, and unmarried or Guardian of her person appointed by the High Court of Chancery and having authority to consent to said marriage". Frances was a minor, aged 18.

Wm Augustus and Frances were married at Holy Trinity Church, Kentish Town, on 18th November 1858. Frances' sister Sarah Hussey was a witness, as was her brother-in-law Thomas Lough. Perhaps rather strange was that none of the Pages were witnesses. Occupations on marriage certificates are often interesting. We know that Thomas Hussey's death Probate gave his occupation as landlord. However, on Frances' marriage certificate he is listed as 'gentleman'. Samuel Page is recorded as Merchant and Broker. William Augustus describes himself as a merchant.

William's mother, Mary Ann, had died earlier in 1858, so William and Frances had only one parent between them – Samuel Page. Even though it seems that Samuel wasn't at his son's wedding he evidently decided to assist his son. As with his older son Samuel, he arranged for him to be admitted as a Freeman of the City of London.

This happened in May 1859. Although Wm Augustus' business wasn't situated within the City of London, he was admitted by 'patrimony' because he was the legitimate son of his father Samuel Page who was himself made a Freeman in 1818. There were advantages to merchants to be a Freeman. A summary is included in Appendix 1.

Initially, they lived near to Frances' sister Elizabeth and Thomas Lough in Hampstead. Elizabeth and Thomas had three young children. In September 1859 Frances gave birth to their first son Harry Ernest. Not long afterwards Elizabeth and Thomas, who was a commercial traveller, moved to Christiania the capital city of Norway, now known as Oslo.

Just over a year after their marriage, Samuel Page died in June 1860. His two unmarried daughters, Eliza and Adelaide needed homes. Wm Augustus and Frances took Eliza into their home and Adelaide went to live with her sister Mary Ann. Wm Augustus and Frances had moved from Hampstead to Godalming and William was now working in the tanning business, as Manager of Godalming Tanning Works. Their second son, William Augustus, was born on 15th April 1861, just two weeks after the census. Therefore, he didn't appear on the census that year. (This sequence of events meant that it took me a long time to locate William Augustus (the second) when I started to find my ancestors.) In November 1861, Wm Augustus was a Trustee of the Marriage Settlement of his sister Eliza to George Goodwin Willis. Then two more children were born in Godalming, Edith Frances in 1863 and Clarence Kirkaldy in 1864. The Kirkaldy name, from Samuel Page's Uncle Adam Kirkaldy and William's brother Adam Kirkaldy (in Australia), was thus carried on for another generation.

Godalming had a Literary Institute, founded in 1859. On a rainy evening in January 1865, the principal residents of the town and neighbourhood gathered at Godalming Public Hall for the Annual Soirée. Wm Augustus was amongst the company of about 50 persons. The platform was decorated with beautiful hot-house plants including an orange tree, which had clusters of fruit hanging from it. They had been lent by R Balchin the Mayor, and G J Hall of Westbrook House. The Mayor was in the Chair and expressed his desire to maintain the present standard of the Institute. There followed an extensive programme, including 'Sing birdie sing' sung by Mrs Alexander Newton; Mr Haydn Harrison played 'Airs from Traviata' as a fantasia. At the interval refreshments were provided by Mr D Norris the local confectioner. The programme continued with many more items, including for example, Mr Dunkley with his entertainment 'Negro Reminiscences' in which "his extreme versatility of genius was fully apparent". He appeared as five distinct characters, each time with a change of dress and sang the following songs: 'Happy may thy dreams be', 'Down among the cotton', 'The Song of Songs', etc with accompaniments upon the piano, concertina banjo, triangle etc and occasionally playing two or three instruments simultaneously. The performance was most loudly applauded, and "Mr Dunkley retired at last amid a perfect furore of applause". After the entertainment concluded Mr Yate proposed a vote of thanks to the Chairman, and after the National Anthem the company retired into the night.

William Augustus was evidently keeping company with the 'respectable' citizens of Godalming. He had a good managerial job and was now the father of 4 small children. The family lived on Brighton Road in Godalming. It seemed that his life was looking good. Oh, how I wish I hadn't thought that! In the *Surrey Advertiser* of 22nd April 1865 there was a column headed:

MAGISTRATES OFFICE – Wednesday 22nd April 1865 (before Duncan Macdonald, Esq)

SERIOUS AFFAIR BETWEEN TWO RESPECTABLE GODALMING TRADERS

Mr Steven Bateman, a local brewer, who had been at the same Soiree as Wm Augustus earlier in the year, was brought up in custody, under a warrant, by Deputy Chief Constable Parr and was charged that on the 10th day of April in the Parish of Godalming he threatened Wm Augustus Page by saying:

"I will give you one of the very damndest thrashings you ever got" and that he put him in fear of bodily harm by such threat.

Oh, my goodness, what on earth was this about? The Magistrate was most anxious that the details of the case should not be aired in court – not washing one's dirty linen in public etc. But both Mr Bateman and Wm Augustus Page were agreeable to the facts being stated in court. I will give a shortened version of the rather wordy newspaper report.

"Wm Augustus Page, tanner of Godalming, was sworn in and stated: "On Monday 10th April the defendant called at my house between 9 and 10 in the evening; my servant came in to me and told me he was there. I was ill, under the doctor's hands at the time with inflammation of the kidneys. The servant came in and said Mr Bateman wanted to see me. I said, 'Ask Mr Bateman into the front room, as I am engaged'.

"When I was disengaged I came out and said 'Mr Bateman, walk in'. He said, 'No I will not, you come out to me'. I said 'No, Mr Bateman, I can't, I'm not well', on which he came in and said, 'You damnation blackguard, how dare you write me such a letter; you only did so to shirk the payment of your bill, knowing that I can't give you the items.' He then afterwards said, 'You damnation thief, if I were such a thief as you I would put my head under the grindstone and grind myself up'."

Good gracious! What language from Mr Bateman. What on earth had passed between them to cause this vitriolic exchange? The cause of the problem is quite difficult to ascertain, but I think that Wm Augustus owed Mr and Mrs Bateman some money. Wm Augustus was further examined and stated:

> "He then shook his fist in my face two or three times, once or twice with his knuckles on my nose. He said he had brought £10 in his pocket and he said: 'Come out you damn cripple and I'll fight you'. He said if it cost him all the money he had, he would give me one of the damndest thrashings I ever had in my life, and that he would stand over me till he could stand no longer."

It is quite difficult to decide whether Wm Augustus was in debt to Mr Bateman, or whether Mr Bateman owed Wm Augustus money, but objected to the demands that Wm Augustus had made. Whatever the origins of the fisticuffs, Mr Bateman was arrested for striking Wm Augustus on the nose. It is not clear exactly what had happened to provoke Mr Bateman. Wm Augustus denied speaking disrespectfully about Mr Bateman, either behind his back or when travelling by train.

Mr Bateman was under the influence of liquor and had thumped Wm Augustus' furniture in a most violent manner. On cross examination Wm Augustus was asked if he had called for a pistol. He replied in the negative and also to the question of "Did you say you would blow his brains out?" Wm Augustus did say that he had lifted up his hands and said that he pitied poor Mrs Bateman.

Mr Bateman had apparently visited Wm Augustus's house a dozen times, which indicates to me that Wm Augustus owed him money. The judge concluded:

> "It appears to me a serious thing to go into a person's house and threaten him with violence – especially in this case where the prosecutor was not an equal to the defendant. I

must call on Mr Bateman to give rather substantial bail – to keep the peace to all Her Majesty's subjects and Mr Page in particular – himself in £50 or a surety of £50. In default of the bail he must go to gaol for 6 months. Mr Joseph Williams of Godalming gave surety of £50."

This was not a very pleasant occurrence and I wondered if it would affect Wm Augustus's standing in the town. In the *Surrey Advertiser* on 1st July 1865 several men were sworn on the Grand Jury, including Wm Augustus, and it appears that they discussed various legal and municipal matters. So, he was still moving in the 'right' circles. However, there were press notifications of his bankruptcy later in 1865.

By 1871 he had moved back to north London. The family was living at 3 Rockhall Terrace, Cricklewood and a son, Stanley Edgar was born there in 1867. His occupation is now 'manufacturing perfumer'. In 1881 he and Frances are still at the same address. This time his occupation is 'commercial traveller'. Two more children had arrived in the household. Kathleen Octavia was born 1st October 1876. (At least she was named after the month in which she was born, as none of the William Augustus's were!) Then came Arthur Claude, the baby of the family, born August 1880.

It is interesting to note that there was a nine-year gap between Stanley and Kathleen. This was very unusual for those times. It is usually suggested that the father must have been absent – in jail or overseas. Neither of these possibilities has shown itself in the records. Possibly Frances had miscarriages?

In 1884 Edith Frances, their eldest daughter, married Mason Gill. On Edith's marriage certificate she gives her father's occupation as 'gas engineer'. William Augustus certainly seemed to have many occupations. Edith and Mason, a Quaker by religion and a dentist by profession, married by licence at St Botolph's Aldersgate, City of London, and set sail for a new life in Philadelphia, USA, with 20 pieces of luggage.

The following year Wm Augustus and Frances' second son, William Augustus, a colour-sergeant in the Kings Own Yorkshire

Light Infantry, married Mary Ann Briggs in Malta. His description of his father's occupation is 'provision merchant'. As already written in the introduction, in 1888 this William Augustus died in Quetta, India, from acute nephritis, three days after his 28th birthday.

By 1991, Wm Augustus and Frances had moved back south of the river and were residing at Bedford Road, Clapham. Wm Augustus describes himself as an invalid supported by relatives. Arthur is the only child at home, he is 10 years old. Also, in the household are their young servant Ada Prew plus two boarders; Charles Chamberlain a warehouseman and Thomas Roberts a clerk, both from Leicester. Times must have been hard, as presumably taking in lodgers was a way of generating income.

In 1895 Edith Frances Gill (née Page) returned to England with her two children. Her daughter, also Edith, but known in the family as Edie, was born in 1885 and Roy in 1887, both in Philadelphia. However, Mason Gill did not return with them and as far as I can ascertain he never again set foot in England. Edith Frances may have come 'home' to help her mother take care of her father, as he was ill. Or she may have 'escaped' from her marriage.

Wm Augustus died, intestate, at his home, 32 Galveston Road, Wandsworth, on the 12th December 1896. He was 60 years old. The cause of his death was obstruction of the bowel.

Chapter 11

Adelaide Page

ADELAIDE, THE YOUNGEST child of Samuel and Mary Ann Page, was baptised at St Mark's Kennington on 21st March 1838. At around this time Samuel would have invested in land in Adelaide, South Australia.

The city of Adelaide was named, with King William IV's consent, for his wife Adelaide in 1836. William, as Duke of Clarence, third son of George III had eight illegitimate children by the actress Dorothea Jordan. These children took the name FitzClarence. Adelaide was a German princess brought over to England to marry William as there was concern about the continuity of the Royal Family. William was 53 and Adelaide 25 when they married in 1818. Adelaide had two daughters who died in infancy and four stillborn babies. Thus, because William and Adelaide could not produce an heir, Queen Victoria came to the throne as the legitimate offspring of William's brother, the Duke of Kent.

Adelaide Page was probably named after both the city and the Queen. One of her Retemeyer cousins was also Adelaide, born 1844, so six years younger than Adelaide Page. As with her siblings there is little information about her schooling or early life. In 1851 she was living with her parents in Lambeth. Seven years later her mother died, when Adelaide was 20. Both she and Eliza were unmarried, so they lived at home to take care of their father. When he died in 1860 the girls were placed with their sibling's households. In the 1861 census Adelaide was living with her sister Mary Ann Blenkarn's family. In 1871 she was with her sister Eliza. In the chapter about Eliza we know that her husband George Willis was absent from home in that year. In 1881 Adelaide had moved in with her brother Samuel. His wife had died in 1873 when his sons were only six and 11 years old. It was good that these boys had their kind Aunt Adelaide come to live with them and take care of them, with their nurse Jane Trott, when they were home for the holidays from boarding school.

We know that she was kind because Samuel said so in his Will: "I give to my sister Adelaide the sum of two thousand pounds absolutely as acknowledgement of her uniform kindness to my relatives."

Samuel died in 1890. Adelaide lived another ten years. She passed away on 14th October 1900. Her address was Gerrard House, 42 Herbert Road, Wimbledon. I think it very likely that Adelaide took care of her money and that she used her inheritance from her brother to buy a bungalow that she could call her own home. It must have been rather wonderful for her, after playing 'musical homes' with her siblings over many years. Her Will is so interesting and reflects her nature. Any debts owing to her are forgiven. Several friends and nieces are each asked to choose a piece of her jewellery as a memento.

She left £100 each to the children of her brother Wm Augustus. She gave her gold watch and her mother's desk to her niece Rose Adelaide Blenkarn, youngest daughter of her deceased sister Mary Ann. She gave £300 to her sister Eliza, and although not mentioned in Adelaide's Will, we know from Eliza's Will that she also received her mother's piano from Adelaide. Her deceased brother Adam's eldest daughter Adelaide married John Ludlow Ffrench in New South Wales. They had a daughter and she was also named Adelaide. As well as being her great-aunt, Adelaide Page was also her godmother. She bequeathed this child £50.

Adelaide requested that her dog be destroyed upon her decease. Any family photos and portraits were to be distributed to her relatives, as her Executors thought fit. The most interesting items in terms of this story are revealed in this passage:

> "Whereas I possess what I call two shares of property in Australia one share having come to me from my father and the other share having been since acquired by me from my brother, I give devise and bequeath one of such shares to my nephew Arthur Claude Page and I give devise and bequeath the other of such shares to my niece Rose Adelaide Blenkarn. "

After all the bequests, the residue of her estate after the sale of her household items and bungalow was to be divided between "my nephew and niece Arthur Claude Page and Rose Adelaide Blenkarn".

The net value of Adelaide's estate was £10,361*. Arthur Claude and Rose Adelaide the youngest children of her brother Wm Augustus and sister Mary Ann, respectively, were now rather wealthy. Moreover, they were each the owners of a one-sixth share of their grandfather's property, Section 8, Goodwood, Adelaide.

Thus, ends Part 1 of this 'Book full of Pages'.

*Allowing for inflation this would approximate to £1,274,400 in 2018.

PART 2

"...heave away, haul away,
for we're bound for South Australia..."

(traditional sea shanty)

Chapter 12

En route to Adelaide

THE ADVENTURE BEGINS.... Ever since I read the newspaper articles about the Page estate being sold in 1917, and the reference to it being akin to 'Jarndyce & Jarndyce' in Bleak House, my interest was stirred. I really thought I ought to try to write a book about the story. In fact, I enrolled in a 'Write your family history' course run by Johanna Moorhead, an author who writes for the Guardian newspaper. There were seven of us on the course at West Dean College in Sussex. We shared our individual stories and were so absorbed in what we each had to tell that we scarcely got around to writing anything! At the coffee break, the whole group said to me, "You HAVE to go to Adelaide!"

Some things are easier said than done. My dear husband, Jeff, had died the previous year. However, my mother was ailing and needed some care. There was no way I could take off to the other side of the world. So, I focused on finding out as much information as I could about the Page family, checking the Wills, trying to piece together the intriguing list of individuals who gained from the sale of Section 8 Goodwood in Adelaide. Some of it made no sense. Who was Rose Phyllis Maud Newnham? At that stage I had not obtained Eliza Willis's Will, so I still hadn't found out the connection.

Early in the summer of 2014 my mother passed away and the next few months were taken up with selling her property and obtaining probate. However, the kernel that was sowed in my mind by my fellow writing course attendees grew into a fully formed plan.

On the 5th November 2014 I flew off to Sydney. I have a habit of trying to kill two birds with one stone. I emailed my old friend and ex-AstraZeneca colleague, Jane Frost, a Sydneysider, and we met up the evening after I arrived. What fun we had, reminiscing and enjoying cocktails, in the Blu Bar, 36 stories up in the Shangri-La Hotel, high above 'The Rocks' where convicts had first been landed in the late 18th century. On one side we looked down onto Circular Quay and on the other to Darling Harbour. It was a fabulous scene and a good way of staving off jet lag.

I slept well and woke early to catch up with emails and make sure that all was well at home in the UK. A message popped up from Ancestry. It so often does! This one asked me how I was related to a particular person. The sender was new to Ancestry and was just getting started but finding it addictive. That is very true, I responded. "I've come halfway round the world to investigate a family court case in Adelaide." The reply I received was quite staggering: "I'm Adam Bough, I emigrated from the UK several years ago and I live in Adelaide". I have come to appreciate that life is full of coincidences, but when I read that message you could have knocked me down with a feather! Adam will feature further on in the story, but now I had to get up and out onto the sunny streets of Sydney. A busy day, starting at the contemporary art gallery seeing some amazing aboriginal art, a brisk walk in the botanical gardens, meandering the craft market on the Rocks, rounded off with a stunning performance of 'La Bayadere' at the Opera House by the Australian National Ballet Company. Sydney Opera House is incredible not only from the outside. The interior is spacious with several theatres, restaurants and exhibition spaces. The theatre seats were upholstered in purple wool, from Merino sheep of course. The jet lag was catching up with me and I had to fight to keep my eyes open for the last act.

Sunday morning was bright and sunny – isn't it always in Sydney? I walked to the Circular Quay and hopped aboard the Manly Ferry. Out onto the harbour with the sunlight reflected on the rippling waves. Past a huge cruise ship moored at The Rocks. Sailing yachts of every size and colour were skimming through the water, avoiding the numerous ferries plying their routes to Taronga Zoo, Manly and Bondi beaches. A slight breeze and bright sunlight, reflective of the expectation ahead.

The ferry unloaded its passengers at the small harbour at Manly, across from the long sandy beach full of surfers. I looked at my map. Head straight off the ferry, past the Sunday market stalls and along Belgrave Street. Past the Manly Oval and turn left onto Raglan Street, heading uphill, then a dogleg turn onto Griffiths Street. Men were doing that Sunday chore of car washing in the heat. Bottle brush plants showed their striking red colour along the kerbside. It was so warm that there was almost a mirage on the wide suburban street. "About a mile walk", I had thought, but it seemed longer. Just when I was thinking I should find someone to ask, I arrived at the south-east corner of Manly Cemetery. It surprised me that it was not enclosed by a wall, like most cemeteries in the UK, but just like a pleasant park, albeit with many gravestones. There were some angelic statues. I passed the area for Roman Catholic burials and then I headed towards Hill Street, which was where the C of E burial area was. I looked at my map again.

I was looking for row B084. Row A was right alongside Hill Street, so I moved one row back and made my way along Row B to grave number 84. Ah, there is was, with a few autumnal leaves scattered on it and the headstone standing parallel to the street:

In loving memory of Martha Page
Died 26th June 1908 aged 67 years

Martha, who had started the court case all those years ago had died 20 years after it began. It would be another nine years before it would be settled. I stood awhile, thinking about Martha and feeling sad that she never saw the results of the court case. She'd had a hard life, was widowed young, brought up five children, ran her own business and struggled along financially. If it hadn't been for Martha trying to obtain her husband's inheritance I would not be standing there. I wonder what she would have thought if she'd known that she was instrumental in bringing her husband's great-great-great-niece half-way round the world to investigate those 'musty court papers'?

I took a photo, then turned and walked back into Manly. I enjoyed a salad lunch and glass of wine, then stood in the sunshine watching surfers on Manly Beach.

Chapter 13

Adelaide

THE FLIGHT FROM Sydney to Adelaide was uneventful. Arriving in a new place is always exciting. The anticipation of what it will be like; will it live up to expectations or will it be a disappointment? Jane had asked me what would keep me in Adelaide for a month. She reckoned that an afternoon would be quite enough time to see the city – but that's a Sydneysider for you!

The taxi dropped me off at The Hilton Hotel, in Victoria Square, in the late afternoon. The hotel was a modern skyscraper, but its footprint was what interested me. Yes, this was Town Acre 335, which Samuel Page had purchased in the 'draw' for land lots in Adelaide in 1837. And I was going to be sleeping on that acre that Samuel never saw, but which his son Thompson Scott had tried to sell in 1850. It seemed very exciting to me, less so to the Receptionist at the hotel, but I did get 'upgraded' to the 10th floor.

The Central Market of Adelaide was immediately behind the hotel. The city, being a 'foody' destination is very proud of the market, so I had my breakfast there the next morning.

Before I ever thought that I would visit Adelaide I had contacted a genealogist in Adelaide. Graham Jaunay had been helpful in providing details of how to access the various archives in South Australia. His help enabled me to send a request, before I left the UK, for the 'musty old papers' to be available for me to review. So it was that after my scrambled egg on sourdough toast and a cappuccino I walked around the corner from the market to the

Probate Registry of the Supreme Court. I identified myself and was handed the papers, given information about where I could work and told that I could not take photographs of the papers.

Oh, the excitement! I couldn't quite believe that after all this time the papers were in my hand. They were tied with faded red ribbon and in a polythene wallet. I left the counter and put the papers on the worktable. Carefully I withdrew them from the wallet and untied the ribbon. Oh no! Oh no! It could not be… This was not the Page vs Page court case of 1888, but some Page vs Page divorce case and nothing to do with Martha or Samuel. These were not my papers! I nearly burst into tears as I carefully gathered them back into the wallet and returned them to the counter. My disappointment was almost overwhelming. What to do now?

After recovering myself, I went to the enquiry desk at the Samuel Way court building, right next door to the hotel. A helpful researcher located the references on his computer for the court case 109, 1888. It had a long title: "Between Thompson Scott Page, Samuel Page, Eliza Willis (formerly Eliza Page), William Augustus Page, Adelaide Page, Willie Parkinson Jay, Edmund Foxcroft Leach and William Henry Grey, Plaintiffs and Martha Page and Samuel Palgrave Page, Defendants." Armed with this information I was able to email the Archive Records and ask for the papers to be sent to the Supreme Court office. I was told that it would take a fortnight for these papers to arrive at the Probate office of the Supreme Court. As this was my holiday as well as my research project, I had booked the Ghan train to Alice Springs and a trip from there to Uluru. I'd hoped that I would complete the Page court case research prior to touring, but it was not to be. I therefore resolved to spend the first week exploring and sight-seeing instead of sitting in the archive office as anticipated.

The first stop, that afternoon, was the South Australian Art Gallery. I had heard that there was a William Morris Gallery there and I've been a fan of William Morris ever since I studied him at school for A-level. An Adelaide family had purchased many original Morris goods, furniture and soft furnishings. The whole of their collection was donated to the Art Gallery. It was filled with wonderful Morris items, together with Lalique and Daum glass, Moorcroft pottery and Liberty Tudric ware. I spent most of the afternoon there.

The city of Adelaide has excellent transport systems. There is a circular bus service which is completely free. The tram runs from the north-west of the city, through the CBD (central business district) out to Glenelg on the coast. The ride is free within the city centre at off-peak hours. At other times the fare was about A$2. The city was very walkable too, so getting around was easy. Despite my disappointment over the papers I was beginning to enjoy myself. Rather ridiculously I was starting to think of Adelaide as my 'second home'.

The next day I boarded the circular bus and fell into conversation with a couple from New Zealand who had driven from Melbourne in a camper van. It's great that you can have interesting conversations, with complete strangers, on a ten-minute bus ride! My destination was the City Archive. I confess to having been rather confused initially. Adelaide, being the state capital of South Australia, is home to a City Archive, a State Archive, a City Library and a State Library. I eventually became familiar with all of them.

The City Archive in Topham Mall was a surprisingly low-key affair. However, it was a treasure trove of photographs of Adelaide through the ages. There were many of Victoria Square, and it was interesting to see horses and carriages on the roads and ladies and gentlemen in Edwardian outfits. There were also some disturbing photographs of trees being felled in Victoria Square, laying it quite bare. I was very pleased to find a photo of the corner of Victoria Square and Grote Street taken in 1929. This was the Town Acre 335, which I knew had been sold out of the family but had not been able to discover exactly when. This photograph showed a two-storey building, called Globe Chambers, with a covered veranda to protect pedestrians and shoppers from the sun.

The caption mentioned Page Street, which was the road at the back of the town acre, off Grote Street, and was named after its original owner. Sadly, it is no longer there, having become part of the Central Market. Globe Chambers in 1929 housed several commercial enterprises, including George Adams' Rich Cakes shop which was next to Turners, who sold ham and cakes. Next door was Tuckers Seedlings and then Rogers Jewellers. The first storey housed, amongst others, E P Rowley, a dental surgeon. Visible in the background of the photograph, on what was originally Town Acre 378, is a very large department store, Moores, which was modelled on Galeries Lafayette in Paris. It is now the site of the Samuel Way Court Building and still features the magnificent central dome.

The archivist was extremely helpful and let me examine lots of books of photographs. Photocopies were charged at only A$1, which I came to realise was a bargain in archival copies! He drew my attention to a large map on the wall that illustrated the District of Adelaide as divided into Country Sections from the Trigonometrical Survey of Colonel Light, the Surveyor General. It had the cartographer's name and date: John Arrowsmith, Soho Square, London, 1839. At the foot of the page was a statement, "Ordered by the House of Commons to be printed 10th June 1841". This was the first map of Adelaide to be published that showed each country section of 134 acres, numbered and with the owner's name. Just south of the central city area, was Section 8 Goodwood, showing S Page's name. I noted that the Brown Hill Creek was running across the north east corner of the acreage. My friendly archivist produced an A2 colour reproduction of the map for me. It is beautiful and now has a special place in my home.

My next stop was the City Library, where the staff were also very helpful, and where I found many useful historical publications. I walked back to Victoria Square in 34 degree heat, lamenting the fact that there were so few trees there now. I emailed a letter to the Adelaide Advertiser to that effect!

The professional genealogist in Adelaide, Graham Jaunay, had told me that he gave Workers' Educational Association (WEA) talks on family history and I was welcome to join his class if it coincided with my visit. That evening I made my way to 223 Angas Street where the WEA classes were held and sat in on Graham's talk. He spoke about family names and their origins, and the challenges of deciphering ancient handwriting, something of which I'd had much painful experience.

I introduced myself to Graham over a cup of tea and he offered me a lift back to my hotel. The group had been complaining about the heat and I began to understand that a temperature of 34 degrees was considered high for Adelaide in the spring. I told Graham about my disappointment with the wrong papers being at the Probate Registry. He suggested that I get in touch with him for any help, after I returned from Uluru.

The next day was very hot again and I kept out of the sun, utilised the hotel swimming pool, and booked myself a coach tour of the Barossa Valley for the following day. The coach headed out of the city to the North East. The temperature had dropped to the mid-20s and was very acceptable. It was good to see the country-side as we headed for the Adelaide Hills. Our coach driver was an excellent guide. We even heard that all the road widths on the original layout of the city were based on multiples of the old 'chain' measurement length of 22 yards. The city was very easy to navigate, being laid out on a grid system.

We headed out to the Barossa Valley and a tour of Jacob's Creek winery. The tasting was educational and included trying a wine in a black glass: we had to identify whether it was a white or red. It was a very enjoyable experience, followed by a delicious lunch at Barossa Chateau, which had a room full of antiques on display. In the afternoon we stopped at Hahndorf, which is a small town of German origin, where beer and bratwurst were much in evidence, and the gift shops were just like those I had seen in Germany. This was certainly a history lesson for me. I had assumed that Australia was colonised only by the British, but there were many early German settlements. The Germans brought their viticulture skills, which is why the South Australian wine is so excellent. I also had a quite a fright when I was buying some cards in a shop. I suddenly noticed a movement in what I thought was the shop assistant's necklace. It was a baby possum in a little bag. Heavens above! Shades of Dame Edna Everage!

The coach driver kindly dropped me off near the hotel and I mentioned that I was doing some family history research and of my connection with the land on which the Hilton Hotel had been built. He said he'd read a letter in the *Adelaide Advertiser* the day before about someone with an interest in the history of Adelaide. That was my letter!

Being a keen maker of patchwork quilts I had planned my visit to Adelaide to coincide with the Adelaide Quilt Show. I was pleased to find that the show was at Wayville Show ground, on the tram route going south and very near to Goodwood Section 8.

There seem to be many coincidences in my life. I'm sure that other people experience these extraordinary happenings, but I was rather surprised by a couple that I'll narrate. On my flight from the UK I read 'The Narrow Road to the Deep North" by Richard Flanagan, an Australian, that had won the Man Booker Prize for 2014. I had heard interviews with Richard Flanagan on the radio and read reviews of the book. His father had been captured by the Japanese in WW2 and forced to labour on the building of the railroad from Siam to India, known as the Burma Railway. He had survived that ordeal. Sadly, he died on the day that Richard finished the book. And here is the first coincidence: Richard Flanagan dedicated his book to his father "For prisoner 335", which was the number given to him by his Japanese captors and the number of Samuel Page's town acre in Adelaide was 335. Part of "The Narrow Road to the Deep North" is set in Adelaide. It is a moving book and I can thoroughly recommend it.

The second coincidence occurred on Saturday morning when I took the tram to Wayville to see the exquisite quilts in the exhibition. There were also many unusual fabrics on the commercial stands. Many of the fabrics for sale in Australia are manufactured in Asia. They generally seemed much brighter than fabrics we get in Europe and that, no doubt, is to do with the sunny climate. I was in the market for a new sewing machine, so spent some time 'test driving' various makes. Eventually I needed a rest, so bought a coffee and joined a couple of ladies at a table. I asked if they had quilts in the exhibition. "Yes" said one lady, whom I later found out was Wendy Thiele from Port Augusta. She had three quilts entered – one was inspired by and made from the fabric in a kimono sent by her grandfather to her grandmother in WW2. He had died working on the Burma railway – another coincidence!

After an inspiring, interesting day at the Quilt Show I returned to The Hilton. Tomorrow I was heading for the Red Centre.

Chapter 14

The Red Centre

I ARRIVED AT THE Ghan station late on Sunday morning. The Ghan is so named after the pioneering cameleers, and their camels, many of whom came from Afghanistan to carry goods and blaze a trail into the hostile outback environment in the 1890s.

However, the long sleek, silver, snake-like appearance of the train looked nothing like a camel. The Ghan is reckoned to be one of the great train journeys of the world. It departs twice a week from Adelaide in South Australia, going up to Darwin in the Northern Territories.

My cabin was very bijou. It had a sumptuous upholstered chair, which later converted to a bed. There was a washbasin, cupboards, and toiletries, everything for an overnight journey. Only a small overnight bag was allowed to be brought to the cabin. Large luggage had been loaded into the luggage vans.

We set off on time at exactly 12.20. A stewardess brought me details of times for my meals and information on some of the train's statistics. They are certainly worthy of sharing. I had noticed whilst waiting on the platform that I could barely see the front or rear of the train. Now I knew why. It is 30 carriages long and has two large diesel locomotives to pull it, which use 40,000 litres of diesel. The locomotives cost A$100,000 to operate and the fees to use the track are A$55,000.

My hostess was one of 30 staff on board and I was in one of the 192 'Gold' cabins. There are also 20 'Platinum' beds, which must be very swish, and about 75 'Red' service seats. There are also the Queen Adelaide Restaurants and Outback Explorer lounges. About an hour after departure and after passing through the suburbs of Adelaide I made my way along to the Queen Adelaide restaurant for lunch. I was presented with a glass of Prosecco in the bar area, then guided to a table and introduced to my dining companions: Tom and Vera, a delightful elderly couple from Melbourne, making a 'once-in-a-lifetime' trip, as indeed most of the passengers were. Flying would be the quicker, cheaper option, but nothing like as much fun.

The lunch was excellent – goats cheese tart with onion jam and rocket leaves, followed by lavender panacotta, accompanied by a glass of chilled Sauvignon Blanc. My 'train facts' guide told travellers that 585,000 dishes are served in the Queen Adelaide restaurants every year. They are washed down with 18,000 bottles of wine and 23,000 cans of coke. The chefs get through 900 litres of virgin olive oil and 25,000 litres of milk. Three thousand litres of water are carried for each carriage.

Enough of stats – let's look out of the window. We had trundled through the northern suburbs of Adelaide and small towns at quite a leisurely pace. It was interesting to see the vehicles that were queueing at the level crossings. "What bad timing", their drivers must have been thinking, as they watched the 30-plus carriages, almost a kilometre long, roll by.

Our first stop was Port Augusta, then we moved on apace and could identify the Flinders range in the distance. The houses were left behind, and we passed farmland and then salt flats as the environment became more hostile and generally scrubland. The few trees were quite stunted. This then was the 'outback'. In the distance I noticed a couple of kangaroos. After Tarcoola, which is the junction with the Indian Pacific railroad that stretches east-west from Sydney to Perth, we passed Woomera, where atomic weapons had been tested many years ago. Coober Pedy, one of the richest opal fields in Australia was off to the east. The townsfolk there live mostly underground, protected from the ferocious heat. Before too long it was time for dinner. Again, good company – some Americans – and later on I returned to my cabin to find my bed made up for the night and my cabin steward asking what time I would like a cup of tea in the morning. This was the life!

My cabin was located on the east side of the train, so the setting sun cast shadows of the train and its wheels on the red earth that we were now passing. It looked very artistic. The train sped on through the night, clocking up some of the total 369,396 kilometres it covers every year between Adelaide and Darwin. This is the equivalent of travelling nine times around the world.

After a good night's rest, I pulled up the window blind at about 5.30am to be greeted by an amazing sunrise. There is something extraordinary about lying in bed moving along at 100km/hr and seeing the scenery whizz past at the dawn of a new day. And the cup of tea was very refreshing.

We were alerted to the 'Iron Man' statue approaching. Surprisingly small, it was erected to commemorate the one millionth concrete sleeper laid on the stretch between Tarcoola and Alice Springs, replacing the wooden sleepers that had been ravaged by white ants and flooding. It was completed in 1980. We were really in the 'red centre' now as we crossed the Finke river. No water in it, of course – just a dry red riverbed. It is apparently the oldest river in the world, the rocky riverbeds dating back 300 million years.

At 13.45 we pulled into Alice Springs station. It had been an exhilarating 25 hours aboard the train. I had read 'A Town like Alice' by Nevil Shute in my teens and it had stuck vividly in my memory, as had the TV series starring Bryan Brown, Helen Morse and Gordon Jackson. I was anxious to hit the town. I had been warned that there was rather a lot of crime in Alice, so I walked from the hotel rather warily. Certainly, there were many drunken Aboriginals lying around on a green space and making rather a lot of noise. It was disconcerting, rather than threatening. I found a couple of good shops, one selling fabric and the other one had some excellent crafts. I bought a couple of metres of fabric but, not being in the market for a didgeridoo, I made my way back to the hotel for dinner. I had an early start the next morning to Uluru.

Distances in Australia are enormous. From Adelaide to Alice Springs it is approximately 1,500 km. From Alice to Uluru is 460km and would take the coach about six hours. It only looks a couple of centimetres on the map! Enroute we had a refreshment stop at Curtin Springs Station on the Lasseter Highway. The station has more than one million acres and mustering the cattle is done by helicopter. It made Samuel Page's 134 acres at Good-wood look rather pathetic. Nowadays at Curtin there is a café, gift shop, petrol station and the opportunity for camel rides, catering for the tourists visiting Uluru and Kata Tjuta. Mount Conner stood majestically in the distance. There was very little traffic on the long straight roads, but the lorries were enormous, towing two, three or more trailers behind them. They are known as road trains.

Desert Gardens Hotel at Ayers Rock, Northern Territories, was my home for the next two nights. We went out to Kata Tjuta, a grouping of 36 domes that were quite mystical. We set off in the heat to walk to the base of Walpa Gorge. Afterwards we went to the Uluru viewing point and watched the fantastical transition of colours as the sun went down, accompanied by a glass of bubbly, enchanted by the oranges, reds, maroons turning to purples and blues. Hundreds of photographs of this amazing sight must be taken every day.

Next day was a very early start at 4.30am to see the sun rise, setting Uluru alight. Afterwards we had a tour of the base of this amazing 'mountain', which is like an iceberg as there is much more of the rock underground than there is above it. We walked to the Mutitjulu Waterhole and saw flora of the region and ancient rock carvings. Afterwards a visit to Kata Tjuta cultural centre to learn more about the aboriginal culture and way of life. The heat was phenomenal, and we had been told to bring a litre of water with us. Fortunately, the coach had water available in a refrigerated tank in the luggage hold, so it was easy to refill our bottles. We arrived back at the hotel by 9.30am, when the temperature was heading towards 40 degrees C.

In the evening there was a 'Sounds of Silence' dinner out in the desert. Aboriginal dancing and didgeridoo playing were the splendid entertainment and the buffet food was delicious. An experienced astronomer was due to give us a talk on the southern sky. I was looking forward to seeing the Southern Cross, but irritatingly the cloud cover was solid. We had to imagine what we might see, whilst the astronomer gave his explanatory talk. It seemed rather hilarious, pretending that we could see the stars, rather like a black comedy sketch.

Next day I flew from Ayers Rock airport back to Adelaide via Alice Springs.

Chapter 15

Adelaide Reflections

FLYING BACK TO Adelaide from Alice Springs I reflected on how air travel has made the world seem a much smaller place. Only 22 hours from the UK and one is half-way around the world in Australia. A couple of hours in the air takes me from Alice Springs to Adelaide, compared with the 24 hours it took on the train.

What of the intrepid emigrants sponsored by the Commissioners of the South Australian Company? Samuel Page had paid his money for his land on the premise that suitable young people looking for employment and adventure would have their passage to Adelaide paid for them. There had evidently been difficulties during the mid-1840s, when the free passage scheme was halted However, I sourced a diary written by Francis Taylor, a young man from Shropshire, recording his voyage to Adelaide on board the *Stag*. His ship left Greenwich with 114 passengers on 11th February 1850. It had a slow voyage down the Thames and along the English Channel to Plymouth where it picked up more passengers. From Plymouth, the ship made one of the fastest voyages recorded under sail from England to Adelaide. Under her master, Captain Baker, the *Stag* departed Plymouth on 8th March 1850 and arrived in Adelaide on 11th June, a total of 95 days. This was quite an exceptional speed, as generally the voyage took 4-5 months. They managed to maintain speeds of 7-8 knots when the wind was good.

There were 257 passengers and 40 crew aboard the *Stag*. The ship was victualled by the Commissioners and there was water and various fresh and preserved foodstuffs, as well as livestock, to last for a voyage of 120 days. There was no intention to put into port enroute, although in previous years some ships had put into Rio de Janeiro and Port Elizabeth in South Africa. Each ship sailing under the rules of the South Australian Company Commissioners carried a surgeon-superintendent to take care of the passengers' welfare. William Thompson was the *Stag's* surgeon-superintendent, although he was not necessarily a surgeon, but according to records did a very good job, was a kind gentleman and looked after the passengers to the best of his ability. However, he was not a miracle-worker – six children and one woman died during the voyage and were buried at sea.

There were 78 children under the age of 18 on board and three more were born during the voyage. One can scarcely imagine the horrors of giving birth aboard a tiny ship tossing around the ocean, with limited medical facilities and equipment. Fifty-one single gentlemen left England that cold February as well as 22 single women and 48 families. Some of the families had 7 children. Just four persons and three children were in the cabin, which was situated above deck or under the poop. This was the equivalent of travelling business or first class. All the others were steerage passengers.

Immigrants to Adelaide needed to be carefully selected and would, no doubt, have to possess skills that were required in the colony, which by this time was 11 years old. On board were many farm labourers. Most of the single young women were domestic servants. There was certainly a variety of skilled workers, including shoemakers, masons, miners, carpenters, bricklayers, blacksmiths, sawyers, grooms, coachmen and a tailor. They hailed from all over the British Isles, from Cornwall to Yorkshire, from Kent to West Meath in Ireland, from Jersey to Middlesex and all points in between. Copper had been discovered in South Australia around 1845, so miners from Cornwall were very welcome.

The *Stag* was a three-masted, square-rigged ship. I couldn't quite image just how small this ship was, crossing 13,000 miles of ocean, so thought it might be useful to do a couple of comparisons. My maternal grandmother's sister emigrated to Melbourne in 1923, on *SS Bendigo*. In Sydney I had seen a huge ocean-going cruise ship, the *Pacific Explorer*. I don't think that anyone travels from the UK to Australia by ship these days except on relaxing holiday cruises aboard enormous liners. I thought it might be interesting to compare the statistics of these three different ships.

Ship/Year	Length (ft)	Beam (ft)	Tonnage	Max Speed (Knots)	Mode
Stag 1850	120	33	678	8	Sail
Bendigo 1923	519	64	13,039	15	Twin screw steam
Pacific Explorer 2014	865	105	77,440	21	Diesel Electric

A quick calculation shows that the Pacific Explorer has a tonnage more than 100 times that of the *Stag*. That little ship sailing to Australia would seem to be the equivalent of taking a rowing boat across the channel. Of course, many people have done this, but I find it incredible that so many individuals took what was a fairly large risk to get to a new life halfway across the world. And Samuel Page's eldest son, Thompson Scott, made the voyage himself in 1849: all the more admirable because his cousin, William Chalmers, the son of Samuel's sister Ann, died at sea on his return from Tasmania in 1848. He was a Lieutenant in the 11th Regiment and in 1845 had sailed to Van Diemen's Land (Tasmania) as the 'guard' of a shipment of about 300 convicts.

What was in store for the passengers of the *Stag* on 9th June 1850 as it sighted Kangaroo Island, the first land they had seen since leaving Plymouth? Kangaroo Island had been the place where the first emigrants settled in 1838, but it was a sand island and they soon went across to the mainland to Holdfast Bay, where

Adelaide was chosen as the place to establish a town. I visited Kangaroo Island. It is amazingly unspoilt. There are a couple of settlements, Kingscote and American River. The ferry from Cape Jervis on the mainland lands at Penneshaw on Kangaroo Island. Many of the roads are unsealed and it would be a very good place to have a 'back to nature' holiday. There are kangaroos and koalas, and no doubt other animals too shy to show themselves during daylight hours. The seals at Seal Bay were fantastic – so many of them – and I walked along the beach where they were sunning themselves, taking care not to get too close. The beach sand was white, the sea the deepest blue and the sky almost the same blue. These colours must have seemed amazing to people arriving from dull old Europe. They certainly impressed me. The eucalypts are lovely trees and would have been totally alien to anyone arriving from Europe. All the vegetation, flora and fauna would have been novel. Nowadays there are organised nature trails, honey farms to visit, emu oil to purchase, small nature parks where injured animals are cared for and visitors can see echidna, emus, cassowary, crocodiles, platypus, pelicans and many other species indigenous to Australia.

The *Stag* did not land at Kangaroo Island but sailed up the Gulf of St Vincent, where they picked up the pilot and made a safe passage to Port Adelaide. The port is about 11 miles from the Adelaide settlement, as it was then, large city as it is now. The settlement's population in 1850 was 15,000 and the colony of South Australia was 60,000. By 1850 a total of 187,000 people had made the journey to the Australian colonies and in the next 10 years 600,000 more made that journey.

Port Adelaide still has a harbour, but there is little shipping these days. There is an excellent maritime museum which I visited. It was full of memorabilia, including a mock-up of a cabin from a ship in the early days of migration. There were models of sailing ships and passenger liners and lots of hands on activities for children. It also had a collection of carved ships' figureheads. I was looking at these when I realised that the one in front of me was of a male figure. This surprised me, as I thought that figureheads were usually female. I looked a little more closely. It was French! That must explain it.

I walked back along the row of figureheads. One was from the barque *Garthneill*. The explanatory plaque indicated that the *Garthneill* was originally named the *Inverneill*. This name rang a bell with me, and here comes another coincidence…

My grandfather's cousin, Roy Gill, born in Philadelphia in 1887, returned to England with his mother Edith Gill (née Page), and was a schoolboy, training to be a seaman on HMS *Worcester*. In 1904 he was an apprentice, sailing to Australia on the barque *Inverneill*!

It was apparently a rough voyage, but it didn't put Roy off as he eventually became Commodore of Ocean Convoys from 1940 to 1945 and was known as the 'most shot-at Commodore in WW2'. He brought all but 34 of 1,869 ships safely into port. In 1941-2 he was also ADC to King George VI. In the 1945 New Year's Honours List he was knighted. Also, in 1945 he was a member of the British Military Court for the trial of war criminals held at the War Crimes Court in Hamburg. Although a very 'honoured' and brave man he was quite ordinary and down to earth. I met Sir Roy as a child at Liverpool docks when we were saying goodbye to his sister, Edie, who was sailing home to Montreal, Canada. In 1957 he was appointed Master of the clipper ship, *Cutty Sark*, in dry dock. He held this appointment until 1965. The beautiful clipper is still in dry dock at Greenwich and is a major tourist attraction.

So, once again I was 'walking on cloud nine' after finding a totally unexpected family link. I caught the train back to Adelaide city centre. I expect that when emigrants arrived in Australia they wanted to have links to home, so many towns have the same names as UK towns. The first station we came to was Cheltenham, then Kilkenny followed by Croydon and Bowden, and the bay at

Port Adelaide is Largs Bay. The train journey from Port Adelaide to Adelaide is like a journey around the UK!

Chapter 16

Goodwood Section 8

IN DECEMBER 1912 and January 1913, the *Adelaide Register* news-paper contained reports of some memories of '50 years ago in Goodwood'.

Samuel and Robert Mills had left their home in Ravenswood, southern Scotland, in December 1838, arriving in Holdfast Bay, Adelaide, in June 1839. They brought seeds from the 'old country' and set about farming in 1840. They rented Adelaide country Section 7 – where Goodwood railway station now stands – from the agent of Jacob Montefiore. They built a small brick cottage at the end of the Reverend Robert Mitchells garden adjoining the Goodwood Road and named it after their Scottish origins. In due course they also put up a cottage alongside the Brownhill Creek on Section 8 for their married ploughman. They had rented Section 8 from the Page family. These two cottages were the only ones that were built to the west side of Goodwood Road at that time.

Around 1844 one of the Page family came to the colony and offered to sell Section 8 to Samuel Mills, but when it came to settling, he was unable to give a good title and the contract fell through.

I wonder if Samuel Mills' son's memory for dates is not very good. Thompson Scott Page arrived in Adelaide in 1849 and certainly was trying to sell Section 8 in 1850, although he had no authority from his father to do so. As we saw in the chapter on

Thompson Scott Page his father Samuel soon removed him from being his agent for collecting rents for his Adelaide property.

However, it seems that the story of Thompson Scott Page trying to 'illegally' sell his father's land is accurate, even if the dates are awry. Samuel Mills' son recalls that his father and uncle grew pie melons that were huge, the size of which he cannot remember seeing since. He and his siblings rolled them a half-mile from the north west corner of the land to their house on Goodwood Road. Ravenswood Farm was their family home for almost thirty years.

The brothers Samuel and Robert Mills also traded as S & R Mills, building contractors. One of their first commissions was the Tavistock Buildings at the east end of Rundle Street, for a Miss Bathgate. Then they built the first United Presbyterian Church in Adelaide, on Gouger Street. They carried on their farming in conjunction with the building business. Certainly, it seems that early settlers worked very hard to succeed in their new country. A little later, in 1865, there was a public house, called The Green Gate Hotel situated on the corner of Park Terrace, Wayville and the Goodwood Road. It had a swinging gate for a sign and carried the homily, "This gate hangs well and hinders none; refresh and pay and travel on".

Although I had stayed at the Hilton Hotel, built on Samuel Page's Town Acre 335 I had not visited his 134-acre country section, Goodwood Section 8. In truth I wasn't exactly sure of the location and just how far it extended. I had been to Goodwood tram stop when I went to the Quilt Show and knew that it must be within the vicinity, but at this point I had still not seen the court papers that would show me the details. I decided to take Graham Jaunay up on his offer to help me. He arranged to meet me at Forestville tram stop, which is about 2 miles from Adelaide city centre, and to drive me around Goodwood Section 8, which is known as Millswood. Knowing now that the Mills brothers farmed the land for at least 30 years it seems fitting that the area should be named after them.

Graham was kindness and helpfulness itself, but I did not have a map of the area and was a bit confused. We drove past the Goodwood Oval and sports grounds. Every small place in Australia seems to have an Oval for cricket. No wonder they field such good international cricket teams. Further on, we stopped and walked across the bridge over the railway. A section of Goodwood Section 8 had been compulsorily purchased by the railway company in 1913 and the monies were paid into the court fund. This was held 'in Chancery' until the court case was finally concluded in 1917. It was interesting to see the railway. I knew about the purchase of this section of the land as I had obtained some papers from the Australian National Archive a few years previously.

The Section 8 area was bounded by East Avenue, oddly enough on the Western perimeter, and by Goodwood Road on the eastern side. The northernmost boundary would be the far ends of the gardens of properties on Chelmsford Avenue and Cranbrook Avenue and the southern boundary was fronted by Lynton Avenue. The railway line had sliced Section 8 into three parts. On the eastern side, the railway line runs diagonally along Arundel Avenue, although, of course, Arundel Avenue was built many years later and fitted alongside the railway line, as did Cromer Parade and Millswood Crescent on the line cutting Section 8 almost in two, diagonally north-east to south-west. The map makes this description easier to understand (see Plate Section 2).

The area was very beautifully kept. Wide avenues with single-storey properties hidden behind established fences, walls and hedges and trees. The Jacarandas were so pretty in their lilac-blue. We don't see Jacaranda trees or eucalypts in the UK, so it certainly felt different to our suburban avenues and roads.

I would love to have knocked on one of the doors to ask if they knew the history of the area, but as I was a guest it seemed impertinent to suggest it. Now that I have a good map of the area that was Section 8, I wonder if the residents of Chelmsford Avenue, Cranbrook Avenue, Allenby Avenue, Curzon Avenue, Fairfax Avenue, Argyle Avenue, Hackett Avenue, Graham Avenue, Meredyth Avenue, Irwin Avenue, Cromer Parade, Millswood Crescent, Lloyd Avenue, Ormonde Avenue, Lynton Avenue, Ravensthorpe Avenue, Arundel Avenue and Grantley Avenue would be curious to know how their properties came into existence. If Google Earth and Google maps are accurate, I think that there are approximately 300 properties in the area.

It does seem rather a shame that there is no avenue named after the Page family. Although there was a Page Street bounding Town Acre 335 in the centre of Adelaide it became subsumed into the Central Market area.

It was a very pleasant drive around the area on a lovely sunny afternoon, and Graham dropped me back near the tram stop and I made my way back into the city centre.

Chapter 17

At last!

FRIDAY THE 28TH November: MOPS day! The Musty Old Papers had arrived at the Probate Registry.

This time there was no mistake. There was quite a bundle of papers and I came to realise that Court Case 109, started in 1888, was closed by the master in 1910 and restarted because so many people had died: they did not know who in the family was entitled to benefit from the sale of Section 8 Goodwood. The second court case was number 356 and lasted from 1910 until 1917. They were tied up with 'red tape', which is actually a faded pink in colour. This ribbon was woven in the Derbyshire town of Wirksworth and was used all over the British Empire.

I carefully unfolded the documents and started to read and take notes. After a while I realised that whilst my reading was up to speed, I couldn't write notes quickly enough. There were so many separate documents containing many pages each that it was extremely difficult to ascertain which ones were relevant. Photography was not allowed, which was rather a blow. I would gladly have paid a fee and been able to photograph the relevant documents, but luckily the Probate Registry did provide a photocopying service.

Before long the documents were tagged with my coloured Post-It flags, identifying the pages that I wanted photocopying. Surprisingly, for Australia, this was not a straightforward process and reminded me of purchasing items in communist Russia. I had to take my photocopying request to the counter, stating the number of pages and the size that I required. I was then given a signed 'chit', confirming my request, which I had to take across Victoria Square to the Samuel Wray courthouse. Down I went into the basement, took a number from the machine, and waited in line until a desk clerk became free and called my number. He then took my chit and, via my credit card, relieved me of quite a large sum of money. I felt very frustrated but realised that whatever the cost of the photocopying it would be less expensive than making a return visit to Australia. My month's holiday was rapidly running out and I needed to get as much information as possible to read at my leisure in my apartment and on my return to the UK. I also had to consider the weight of all the paper that had to be flown home. I returned to the Probate Registry with my invoice and photocopying could commence. In total the photocopying clerk made 33 x A4 copies and 46 x A3 copies for me. I've tried hard to forget the cost, which was somewhere in the region of A$300.

The frontispiece to the Court Case of 1888 read as follows:

South Australia in the Supreme Court No 109 of 1888
Between: Thompson Scott Page, Samuel Page, Eliza Willis (formerly Eliza Page) William Augustus Page, Adelaide Page, Willie Parkinson Jay, Edmund Foxcroft Leach and William Henry Grey, Plaintiffs and

Martha Page and Samuel Palgrave Page, Defendants.

Many of the documents were affidavits for striking out and substitution of parties. This was why the court case had gone on so long. Any slight change was a reason for the lawyers to produce volumes of paperwork. I am sure that anyone in the legal profession would be able to explain the justification of this to me, but it seemed to be bureaucratic mumbo-jumbo.

The Court Case 356 was similar but, unsurprisingly, listing different names.

Samuel Palgrave Page, Robert Palgrave Page, Alfred Samuel Page, Clara Page, Arthur Claude Page and Rose Adelaide Blenkarn, Plaintiffs

And

William Stonhewer Freeman, Cecil William Sawyer Marshall, Catherine Agnes Young, Gertrude Mary Mulford and Rose Phyllis Maude Peyton (formerly Rose Phyllis Maude Newnham, an infant but now of full age)

And

Charles Wilcox a person served with Notice of Judgment and who has entered an appearance.

So, the persons listed in court case 356 are totally different from the ones listed in court case 109.

One beautifully hand-written document was from Rose Phyllis Maude Newnham's father, which read:

I, Charles Edward Newnham of Ringwood in the County of Hants, solicitor, make Oath and say as follows:

1. I am the father of the above-mentioned infant Defendant Rose Phyllis Maude Newnham who is at present residing with and under the care of her Uncle, Colonel Arthur Newnham at Jullunder Cantonment, Punjab India.

2. The said infant Defendant was born on the 12th day of April 1891 at Bristol in the County of Gloucester.

3. The said infant Defendant has no friends or relations to my knowledge resident in the State of South Australia.

One piece of information I was very pleased to discover was that Samuel Palgrave Page must have taken up the case originally in 1888 on behalf of Martha Page, Adam Kirkaldy Page's widow. When I visited her grave in Manly, I felt rather upset that she had been widowed for a long time and had not received her husband's inheritance. However, it seemed when reading the court papers that Samuel Palgrave Page had stepped in and given her the monies to which she was entitled in return for her share of Section 8. I was reassured to read that information.

It would take a greater brain than mine to understand all the documentation. In fact, it had taken the best legal brains some 29 years to sort it all out. Although I was most interested in the outcome, there were some interesting documents. The 'List of Documents comprising Title' totalled 52 in number on the first two pages of lists, starting on 1st April 1839 up until August 1895. There were more, but I did not have a photocopy of the whole list.

Mr Justice Buchanan was the 'Master' who finally got a grip of the whole debacle. In the copies that I have of court case 356 there are his scribbled pencil notes in the margins. They reduce hundreds of pages of legalese to a couple of pages of his succinct comments on the whole case. Here follows the simplified table from the MOPs, which explains some of the events and the dates on which they took place. This table is a summary within the papers of all the actions that had taken place.

SAMUEL PAGE – died 4th June 1860

By Will appointed Executors Benjamin Colaco and Samuel Page the Younger and devised and bequeathed property from and after death of wife among children living at wife's death as tenants in common.

Thompson Scott Page, died 23 March 1872

23 April 1861

Assigned his share to Samuel Page the Younger upon Trust, after the death of himself and his wife, for all his children on reaching the age of 21, in equal shares.

31 December 1883

Willie Jay and Edmund Leach were appointed Trustees in place of Moon to act jointly with Samuel Page the Younger.

24 August and 1 October 1888

TS Page, AS Page and WA Page (sons) released Trustees in respect of certain property which had been sold.

TS Page (senior) and spouse both died prior to 20 Nov 1905.

Three children, Thompson Scott Page, Plaintiff,
Alfred Samuel Page, Plaintiff,   William Augustus Page

(died 28 October 1901) having previously attained 21 by Will gave Estate to his wife Clara (Plaintiff) his sole Executrix.

20 November 1905
W Jay and E Leach surviving Trustees conveyed unto three plaintiffs above named as tenants in common.

2 June 1914
Thompson Scott Page (younger) assigned his share to Charles Wilcox absolutely.

Mary Ann Page (Blenkarn), died 28 September 1879

20 May 1848
By Indenture (being ante-nuptial Marriage Settlement) Mary Ann Page assigned to John Blenkarn and Samuel Page the Younger as Trustees her interest in testator's ante-nuptial Marriage Settlement of 25/4/1823.

3 November 1852
F France appointed Trustee in place of John Blenkarn

26 October 1861
By Indenture between Samuel Page the Younger and F France as Trustees of 1st part, Testator's executors of 2nd part, A Blenkarn and MA Blenkarn (above) his wife 3rd part.

Testator's Other Children:
W A Page, A Page, S Page the Younger, Eliza Willis,T S Page,
A K Page

Trustees of Settlement of 23/4/1861:
S Page & F Moon

Trustees of Testator's Ante-nuptial Settlement:
A Johnson, W H Grey

In which recited Testator indebted to Trustees of his Marriage Settlement in sum of £12,714. Testators children desirous sale of estate in Australia should be indefinitely postponed.
It was agreed in consideration of payment of £671, parties of first three parts released parties of 5th part from sum of

125

£12,714 and the parties of the 5th part by direction of parties of 1st four parts did release parties of 2nd part from the £12,714.

Eliza Page (Willis), died 14 February 1906

31 October 1861

On her marriage assigned her share to Ralph Goodwin and Samuel Page the Younger upon trust after death of survivor or children of marriage for persons as she shall appoint Power to sell Estate.

4 September 1863

Wm A Page(brother) appointed in place of R W Goodwin with Samuel Page the Younger.

27 November 1901

Stonhewer Parker Freeman and Henry Stonhewer Freeman (Defendants) were appointed Trustees in place of Samuel Page the Younger and Wm A Page who had died.

14 February 1906

Eliza Willis (survivor) died. No children of marriage.
By Will of Eliza Willis exercise of power gave property to her Trustees Cecil Wm Sawyer, Catherine Agnes Marshall and Gertrude Mulford (defendants) with full power to settle accounts with Trustees upon trust after debts etc and certain items in trust for Rose Phyllis Maude Newnham (Defendant) (an infant) absolutely.
Will approved in England. Exemplification sealed on 16 July 1907 in SA.

William Augustus Page, died 12 December 1896

Mortgaged share to Samuel Page the Younger.

6 July 1865

Conveyed his one-sixth share and all the other share of him including his part share of the one-seventh share of M A Blenkarn purchased for benefit of six other children to Adelaide Page her executors administrators and assigns.

Adelaide Page, died 14 October 1900

By Will devised her share and her share acquired from Wm A Page one of such shares to her nephew Arthur Claude Page (Plaintiff) and other to her niece Rose Adelaide Blenkarn (Plaintiff)

Will proved in England by MLP Crozier and LG Humphreys the Executors.

Exemplification sealed in SA on 19 February 1904.

Samuel Page the Younger, died 26 December 1890

Will devised all real Estate (except that over which he had a general or special power of appointment) unto his two sons Samuel Palgrave Page and Robert Palgrave Page (Plaintiffs) as tenants in common.

Will proved in England 19 February 1891 and Exemplification sealed in SA on 19 February 1904.

Adam Kirkaldy Page, died 23 June 1874

Leaving widow Martha Page and five children: A E Page, A R Page, Wm A Page, F Page, A M Page.

25 May 1890

Letters of Administration were granted to J T Hackett as attorney for Martha Page.

26 December 1892

F A Worth (the Mortgagee) by direction of Martha Page (widow) and A E Page (now French), A R Page, W A Page, F Page (four children) and the said J T Hackett conveyor all share of F A Worth (as Mortgagee) and of the four children above mentioned in residuary Estate of Testator including their shares of the one-seventh share of the said Mary Ann Blenkarn purchased for the benefit of the six other children of the Testator to the Samuel Palgrave Page.

20 August 1895

A M Page (other child) and the said J T Hackett as Administrator conveyed share (as Above) of the said A M Page to the said Samuel Palgrave Page (Plaintiff).

Some of the table is less easy to understand, especially the role of the numerous Trustees, Executors and Assignees. I spent some time working out who owned what, at what time, and how that outcome had been derived. I made my own table, indicating who owned how much of Goodwood Section 8, and at what time. I also list the events that took place to change or realign the ownership. Writing the outcomes in tabular form greatly helped my under-standing of how the original owners, after the death of their father in 1860, morphed into the actual beneficiaries after finalisation of the court case in 1917.

1860

Section 8 Goodwood Adelaide, The Page Estate, left by Samuel Page (1796-1860) equally to his seven children:

Thompson	Samuel	Mary Ann	Eliza	Adam K	William A	Adelaide
1/7th	1/7th	1/7th	1/7th	1/7th	1/7th	1/7th

1861

26th October – Mary Ann's share bought out by her siblings. Mary Ann received £671. 9s. 10d

Thompson	Samuel	Mary Ann	Eliza	Adam K	William A	Adelaide
1/6th	1/6th	1/6th	1/6th	1/6th	1/6th	1/6th

1865

William Augustus (bankrupt) sells his share to his sister, Adelaide

Thompson	Samuel	Eliza	Adam K	Adelaide
1/6th	1/6th	1/6th	1/6th	1/3rd

1872

Thompson Scott Page dies. He leaves his one sixth share to his three sons, Thompson Scott the Younger, Alfred Samuel and William Augustus.

Thompson	Alfred S	William A	Samuel	Eliza	Adam K	Adelaide
1/18th	1/18th	1/18th	1/6th	1/6th	1/6th	1/3rd

1873

Adam Kirkaldy dies intestate – his widow is Martha Page – she takes his share.

1888

Commencement of court case 109 – Martha claims Adam's share of his father's estate.

1890

Martha is granted Letters of Administration (this is granted when there is no Will). Samuel Page dies and leaves his one-sixth share to his two sons, Samuel and Robert

Thompson	Alfred S	William A	Samuel P	Robert P	Eliza	Martha	Adelaide
1/18th	1/18th	1/18th	1/12h	1/12th	1/6th	1/6th	1/3rd

1892

Samuel Palgrave Page buys out Martha's and her children's share.

Thompson	Alfred S	William A	Samuel P	Robert P	Eliza	Adelaide
1/18th	1/18th	1/18th	1/4th	1/12th	1/6th	1/3rd

1894

William Augustus, son of Thompson Scott the Elder, dies and leaves his share to his wife Clara.

Thompson	Alfred S	Clara	Samuel P	Robert P	Eliza	Adelaide
1/18th	1/18th	1/18th	1/4th	1/12th	1/6th	1/3rd

1900

Adelaide dies. Leaves her two shares to nephew Arthur Claude Page and niece Rose Adelaide.

Thompson	Alfred S	Clara	Samuel P	Robert P	Eliza	Arthur C	Rose A
1/18th	1/18th	1/18th	1/4th	1/12th	1/6th	1/6th	1/6th

1906

Eliza Willis (nee Page) dies. Leaves her share to Rose Phyllis Maude Newnham – not a relative and who was under 21 years of age.

Charles W	Alfred S	Clara	Samuel P	Robert P	RPM Newnham	Arthur C	Rose A
1/18th	1/18th	1/18th	1/4th	1/12th	1/6th	1/6th	1/6th

1910

Court case restarted. Thompson Scott Page the younger assigns his 1/18 share to Charles Wilcox (not a relative) in 1911.

Charles W	Alfred S	Clara	Samuel P	Robert P	RPM Newnham	Arthur C	Rose A
1/18th	1/18th	1/18th	1/4th	1/12th	1/6th	1/6th	1/6th

1917

Court case resolved and the recipients received these approximate amounts – there is no clear allocation listed anywhere in the court papers.

Charles W	Alfred S	Clara	Samuel P	Robert P	RPM Newnham	Arthur C	Rose A
£1222	£1222	£1222	£5500	£1833	£3666	£3666	£3666

At last I had the final allocation of the estate, decided in April 1917. The land was put up for sale by public tender. Amazingly, there was another fiasco around the sale of the estate. Tenders were received by 22nd June in sealed envelopes; they were then held for a fortnight, when the names and prices were made public. This was apparently to allow the army or the government to put in a bid as there was an idea that the land could be used for homes for war widows. The bid by the government was slightly higher than the bids already received in sealed envelopes. There was an absolute outcry and so the land was offered again. The Supreme Court accepted a tender from Messrs Charles Irwin, W B Wilkinson and A C Catt for just over £25,000 and a company was formed with the intention of putting most of the site on the market immediately.

In September there was an advertisement in *The Register* extolling the virtues of the site, before the sale of 212 building lots on Saturday 22nd September. The advertisement refers to the land as the Millswood estate, rather than Goodwood Section 8, and it reminds readers that it is in direct communication with the sea on the Brighton Railway and the hills on the Melbourne line. This would be an absolute boon for anyone with a young family, for rather than taking the family into the city centre before setting out for the day, they could go directly from where they lived, via the Millswood or Clarence Park stations.

The directors of the company were determined to make it a first-class residential suburb. No business premises of any description would be permitted and building restrictions would be imposed for the benefit and protection of purchasers. Three acres in the centre of the site would be reserved for recreation grounds. A competition, with a £25 prize, for the design of the clubhouse, was mooted, to include surroundings of a bowling green, croquet lawn and tennis courts. All designs were to be displayed and the winning design will be shown in the Adelaide Mail. The directors were resolved to make Millswood attractive to the right class of people, and those contemplating the purchase of allotments there could feel confident that the neighbourhood would, for all time, be most desirable and select.

Having explored the area with Graham Jaunay I can vouch for it being an extremely attractive area in which to live.

It was nearly time for me to leave Adelaide, but first I had a date to keep with Adam Bough, whom I had first encountered via Ancestry when I was in Sydney. We had sent a few messages in the ensuing weeks and were determined that we should meet up in Adelaide. We thought that Adam's great uncle and my grandfather's cousin's husband might be one and the same person. They had the same name. On the 25th November a young cricketer by the name of Phillip Hughes was batting in the Sheffield Shield for New South Wales against South Australia. A bowled ball hit him in the neck, and he died two days later of a sub-arachnoid haemorrhage. It was a shocking death and in the news for days. His funeral service on 3rd December was relayed to Sydney cricket ground and to the Oval in Adelaide.

Adam and his wife Debbie were keen cricket fans and planned to be at the Oval. Why not meet me for coffee, en route? So it was that I arrived at Treasury 1860, a very nice bar and restaurant on King William Street, a couple of blocks from where I was staying. Adam and Debbie arrived and we laughingly told each other tales of how our families had given us warnings about 'talking to strangers' – for me from my children and for Adam from his mother. It turned out that we didn't have two heads, nor horns, and we got on like a house on fire! The coffees turned into beers and we could probably have chatted for several hours, but they remembered that they needed to be at the Oval to see the televised funeral service, so we parted hastily with promises to keep in touch – which we have done!

Eventually, we discovered that the relative whom we thought we shared was not one person but two, but nevertheless we have kept in touch and perhaps one day I'll visit Adelaide again and be able to spend more time with Adam and Debbie. Meanwhile Facebook works quite well.

The last few days in Adelaide flew by. Jamie Oliver had just opened a new restaurant in an old bank building on King William Street, so I ate there a couple of times and really enjoyed the vibe and chatting to other folk trying out the new restaurant.

I'd been away for over a month and was looking forward to getting back to the UK and seeing my family, but was extremely sad to be leaving the lovely city of Adelaide. When I'd been researching in the City Archive I found a postcard with a poem entitled 'Adelaide'. It captured my imagination and seems to be an appropriate epitaph to my sojourn in South Australia.

Adelaide
(composed by H M Bidmeade)

I have gazed on other cities
When the lights were all agleam
I've climbed the highest mountain
And paddled the longest stream
Yet search the world all over
No matter where one goes
You'll find joy and beauty in the city,
where the River Torrens flows

Adelaide! Adelaide!
You're the grandest place of all
Wherever I be, on land or sea
I'll answer to your call
Adelaide! Adelaide
Where the sunshine always beams
You're calling me, a wanderer
To the city of my dreams

There is beauty in your gardens
There is glory in your trees
The sunny beaches are the finest
They are washed by southern seas
So loudly raise your voices
To all the world disclose
There's a city grand in Aussie land,
where the River Torrens flows.

Hilton Hotel, Adelaide, in 2014. It was built on Town Acre 335.

Town Acre 335, Grote Street, and Victoria Square in 1929. Page Street is on the right-hand side.

B 5153

Summary

South West corner of Grote Street and Victoria Square, 27 March 1929. On the right is Page Street. Where the gap occurs in the verandah a shop front was installed and the verandah made continuous in 1929. George Adams Limited Rich Cakes stands next to Turner's sellers of ham and cakes. Next door to this is Tuckers Seedlings and then Rogers Jewellers. The first storey of this building (Globe Chambers) houses among others, EP Rowley dental surgeon and James A Gibson. The Moores department store can be seen behind the building in Victoria Square.

Victoria Square, Adelaide looking directly towards the Supreme Court.
Town Acre 335, with two-storey building, is on the right.
This photo is from the Edwardian era.

Probate Registry , King William Street, Adelaide,
where I was able to view the 'Musty Old Papers'.

En route to Alice Springs – The Ghan and me.

The *Garthneill* figure head in
Port Adelaide Marine Museum.
Formerly *Inverneill* figure head, in which
Roy Gill sailed to Australia as an
apprentice, in the early 1900s.

Sir Roy Gill, 1887-1967. ADC to King
George VI, Commodore of WW2 Atlantic
Convoys; Commodore of the *Cutty Sark*,
Greenwich. Sir Roy was a cousin of
William Augustus Page.

The railway line that cuts through Goodwood Section 8.

An avenue of jacaranda trees at Goodwood Section 8,
now known as Millswood, 2014.

The 'Musty Old Papers' in 2014. They had probably lain untouched in the archives since 1917.

Montague Chambers, London Bridge, Southwark, London. This was the office of Samuel Page and Son in the first quarter of the 20th Century.

The late SAMUEL PALGRAVE PAGE, J.P.

Samuel Palgrave Page 1861-1937. The portrait was painted in 1912 by Edward Parry and was published in this form to accompany his obituary.

Apprentice indenture for Alfred Samuel Page, for Gold-smiths Livery Company.

This Indenture Witnesseth That *Alfred Samuel Page son of Thompson Scott Page late of Melrose Hall Putney in the County of Surrey Gentleman deceased* doth put himself Apprentice to *Samuel Page of Nº 16 Water Lane Tower Street in the City of London Provision Merchant* a Citizen and Goldsmith of *London*, to learn his Art of a *Provision Merchant* and with him, (after the manner of an Apprentice) to serve from the day of the date of these Presents, until the full End and Term of Seven Years, thence next ensuing, to be fully complete and ended. During which Term, the said Apprentice his said Master faithfully shall serve, his Secrets keep, his lawful Commands every where gladly do. He shall do no Damage to his said Master, nor see it to be done by others ; but that he to the best of his Power shall let, or forthwith give Warning to his said Master of the same. He shall not waste the Goods of his said Master, nor lend them unlawfully to any. He shall not commit Fornication, nor contract Matrimony, within the said Term. He shall not play at Cards, Dice, Tables, nor any other unlawful Games, whereby his said Master may have any Loss. With his own Goods, or others, during the said Term, without Licence of his said Master, he shall neither buy nor sell. He shall not haunt Taverns nor Playhouses, nor absent himself from his said Master's Service by Day nor Night unlawfully; but in all things, as a faithful Apprentice, he shall behave himself towards his said Master, and all his, during the said Term. And the said Master, in consideration of the Premises

his said Apprentice, in the said Art which he useth, by the best means that he can, shall teach and instruct, or cause to be taught and instructed; finding unto his said Apprentice, Meat, Drink, Apparel, Lodging, and all other necessaries, according to the Custom of the City of *London*, during the said Term. And for the true performance of all and every the said Covenants and Agreements, each of the said Parties binds himself unto the other by these presents. *In Witness* whereof, the said Parties to these Presents have hereunto interchangeably set their Hands and Seals, the *seventh* — Day of *April* — in the *thirty eighth* — Year of the Reign of our Sovereign LADY VICTORIA, by the Grace of God of the United Kingdom of *Great Britain* and *Ireland*, Queen, Defender of the Faith, and in the Year of our Lord one thousand eight hundred and *seventy five.*

Sealed and Delivered }
in the Presence of

J H Williams
Goldsmiths' Hall

Alfred Samuel Page

☞ This Indenture must be immediately enrolled at the *Chamberlain's Office*, in *Guildhall*.—And on the Death or Change of Master, the Apprentice must come to *Goldsmiths' Hall*, to be TURNED OVER to the Executor or new Master, and afterwards attend at *Guildhall* to be registered, or he will lose his Freedom.

Note. By an Act of Parliament every Indenture, Covenant, Article, or Contract, must bear Date the Day it is executed; and what Money or other Thing is given or contracted for with the Clerk of Apprentice, must be inserted in words at Length; otherwise it will be void, the Master or Mistress forfeit Fifty Pounds, and another Penalty; and the Apprentice be disabled to follow his Trade, or be made Free.

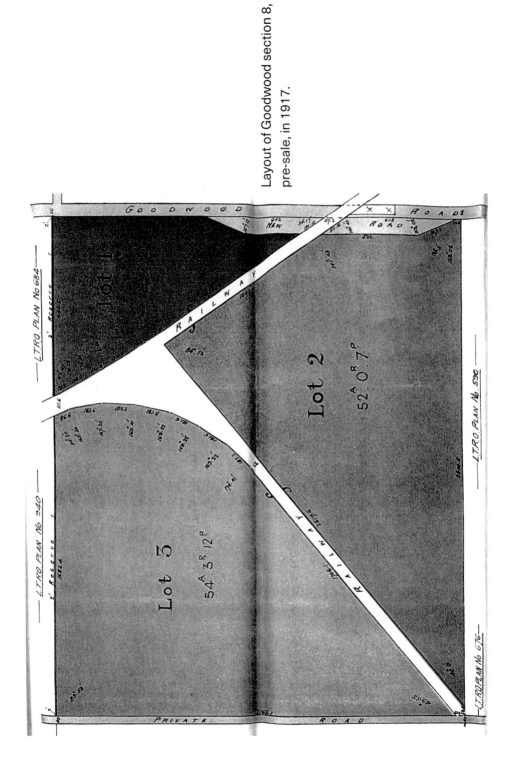

Layout of Goodwood section 8, pre-sale, in 1917.

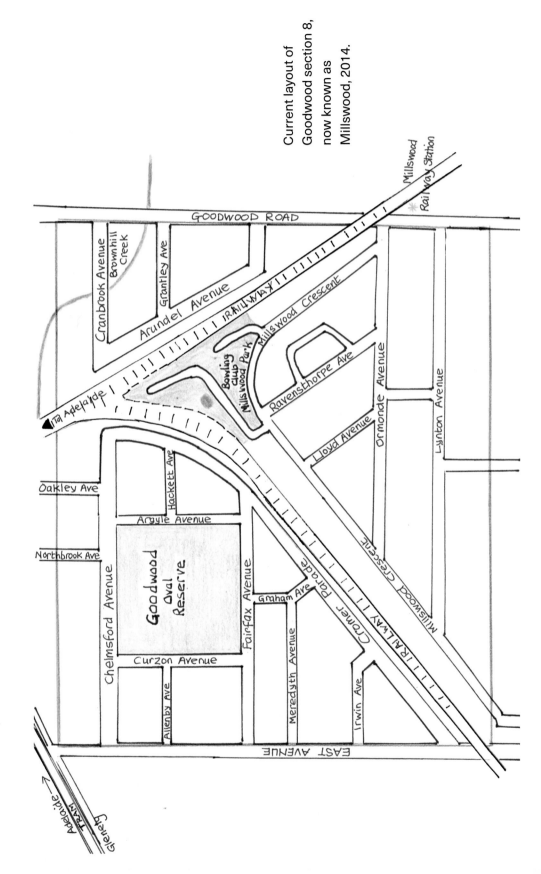

Current layout of Goodwood section 8, now known as Millswood, 2014.

The Family Hotel, in Bega, owned by James Rixon in 1859.

Bega Cheese – sold in Australia today.

PART 3

The Recipients

I had researched the family history for something like ten years. My brother was always asking me, "have you found the money"? It was a joke, but I had found the family money in Australia, of which we Pages living in the UK in the 21st century knew nothing, and certainly hadn't inherited any of it.

After I returned from Adelaide I was able to look through all the photocopies from the Probate Registry at my leisure. I knew something about some of the recipients but could now spend time researching them in more detail and finding out what happened to their inheritance. Did they spend it in one go, invest it wisely, leave it to their children? Did it bring them happiness?

Chapter 18

Thompson Scott Page the younger
(my first cousin three times removed)

Thompson Scott Page was born on 6th February 1853 'on the Sturt', Adelaide. He and his parents returned to the UK when he was one year old. When his father became paralysed, he was sent out to Australia to live with his Uncle Adam. Within a couple of months of his arrival he was trifling with gunpowder, which exploded and he had to have two fingers amputated.

Although he was not on the final list of recipients of the sale of Goodwood Section 8, it is worth briefly looking at what happened to him. He moved from Merimbula, to Hay, Riverina. He was still in New South Wales, but a considerable way inland. In 1880 he married Clara Margaret Mallagh. They had five children: Alice Ellen, William Thompson, Lena Clara, Bertha Adelaide Ita and Olive Belle. Alice died in infancy.

In 1890 Clara died at the age of 32, leaving Thompson to look after four small children. He was soon looking for another wife and in June 1891 he married Anastasia Marie Fleury. Sadly, that marriage only lasted two and a half years, as Anastasia died in January 1894, aged 43. There were no children of that marriage, but I do wonder if Anastasia died in childbirth, which was very common in that era.

It wasn't too long before Thompson was seeking his third wife. He found her in one of Anastasia's nieces. Agnes Lyster was 17 years younger than Thompson. They were married in 1896 and their firstborn son, Alfred Scott Lyster, was born that year. He was followed by a further six siblings; Hilda Muriel, Frederick, Dorothy Daisy Sealy, Maud May, Marie Therese and Sylvia Cecilia. Frederick died in infancy. Thompson then had 10 children who were living. However, there was a wide spread of ages. William Thompson was born in 1892 and Sylvia Cecilia in 1913, so there was 21 years between the oldest and youngest.

In 1894 and 1896 Thompson Scott Page was mentioned in the *Government Gazette* as being the licensee of the Court House Hotel on Lachlan Street in Hay. In August 1895 he was summoned at the instance of Senior Constable Fortescue and Constable Moody of Hay Police for keeping his licensed premises open for the sale of liquor during prohibited hours. He was fine £5 and costs. It is recorded that he paid.

In December 1897 he was living in the Fitzroy region and is mentioned in the rate book for that area – he had paid his rates. There is little mention of him until 1911 when he must have been very hard up and sold his one-eighteenth share of Goodwood Section 8 to Charles Wilcox, for £200. That transaction must have been one of the best that Charles Wilcox ever made, as the value of his one-eighteenth share after the sale in 1917 was £1,222, a 600% return in just six years.

In the 1913 census the family was living at 59 O'Grady Street, Albert Park, Melbourne and Thompson's occupation was listed as 'labourer'. How different his life had become, compared with his brother Alfred Samuel.

Just one year after his last child Sylvia was born Thompson Scott Page died in 1914. He was 61 years old. On the 29th September 1914 there was a death announcement in *The Age*, a Melbourne daily newspaper.

> PAGE – on 28th September at 59 O'Grady Street, suddenly, Thompson Scott Page, dearly beloved husband of Agnes Page, loving father of Willie, Daisy, Mrs A Clark, Mrs E Smith, Alfred, Hilda, Dorothy, Marie, Sylvia and beloved

and only brother of A S Page, Montague Chambers, London-bridge.

In due course probate was listed in the press; Thompson Scott Page had left the grand total of £7. I expect Agnes struggled on, and I hope that some of her children looked after her. I have some indication of their marriages and children, and there are some great-grandchildren of Thompson's living in Australia today. Perhaps we will eventually make contact.

Of Charles Wilcox, being a non-relation, I know nothing.

Chapter 19

Alfred Samuel Page
(my first cousin, three times removed)

ALFRED SAMUEL WAS the second son of Thompson Scott and Helen Page. He was born in Orpington, Kent in October 1855. His older brother had been born in Adelaide and they had a younger brother, another William Augustus who was born in 1857. At some stage their father Thompson Scott became paralysed and lived in an institution, Melrose Hall in Putney. In 1871 Alfred and William were living with their mother at Stratford Grove in Putney with a lady called Lydia Chaplin. Also living there was Louisa Jones, who was a governess. Helen Page is listed as a 'fundholder', which generally means that there is some investment on which she is living.

Ten years later, Alfred aged 25 and William aged 23 are still living at home with Helen and are both commercial clerks. Helen is now widowed, and they have moved across the river to Hackney. They have an eighteen-year-old domestic servant called Mary Allen.

In 1875, at the age of 21, Alfred was apprenticed to his uncle Samuel Page. This is a very odd age to be apprenticed. He had been working as a commercial clerk since he was 15. The apprenticeship would mean that he could become a Freeman of the City of London. I feel sure that his uncle arranged this, because the only other way to become a Freeman was by Patrimony, and his

141

father had died in 1872. Uncle Samuel had taken the son of his elder brother under his wing.

Alfred married Edith de Morel Warnington, on 21st April 1883 when he was 28. Edith was 23. They were married at Stoke Newington and made their home at East End House, Finchley. It was a substantial house of 14 rooms. Four days after their first wedding anniversary Edith gave birth to their only child, a son, baptised Charles Carew.

Alfred worked with his uncle Samuel at Water Street near to the Tower of London. Also working for the merchant brokers Samuel Page & Son was Samuel's son, Samuel (Palgrave). They eventually moved over the river to Montague Chambers on Tooley Street, right next door to Southwark Cathedral. The area is known as London Bridge and Montague Chambers is still in existence. Charles Carew also came into the company, working with his father and his father's cousin; his great-uncle Samuel having passed away in 1890.

An article in the *Freeman's Journal* in Sydney in 1894 gives information about butter that was exported to London. The total imports to the UK for the week ending 9th December were 46,868 cwt (hundredweight), against 39,488 cwt for the corresponding week of 1892. Samuel Page were always quoted as the London brokers/agents giving the market butter prices. That week they quoted Australia & New Zealand finest 116s to 120s; good to fine 100s to 114s; medium 90s to 96s and inferior 70s to 80s per cwt.

Samuel Page and Son were the premier brokers of butter and cheese from all over the world: principally for Australian and New Zealand butter, but also for imports from the continent and the USA. This meant that they were, as Alfred Samuel Page said, "brokers pure and simple and had never owned a farthing's worth of butter in their lives". The company advised dairy manufacturers to avoid selling to speculators, who would take some of their profit.

However, being brokers pure and simple did leave them open to taking responsibility for actions that were not of their making.

An article published in the *Otago Witness* (New Zealand) on 12th May 1909 illustrates what could happen to perfectly innocent parties. I summarise it:

Samuel Palgrave Page, Alfred Samuel Page and Charles Carew Page were summoned for importing butter into the United Kingdom which contained more than 16% of water. This was the top legal limit allowed. Four containers of butter that had arrived at Parkeston Quay, Harwich addressed to Samuel Page & Co was tested by HM Customs. They were found to contain excess water to the tune of 4.9, 4.5, 4.7 and 2.1 per cent. The fault was in fact due to the shippers on the continent, but they were beyond the magistrate's jurisdiction. So, as they could not get to the consignors, the consignees had to be made responsible. Mr F F Fox, Chief Inspector of the Metropolitan Police, visited Mr Alfred S Page and told him about the butter and the results of the analysis by HM Customs. Alfred Page showed him a copy of a telegram sent to a firm in Budapest stating that, owing to the excessive amount of water in the butter it could not be sold in England. Mr Page said that although he accepted responsibility as consignee, he did not see how they could be held responsible. The defendants' firm was one of very high repute. Their business consisted of receiving goods from people abroad and selling them in London, charging a commission for doing so.

Regarding the present case they had received a letter on 19th January from the Hungarian Butter Company saying that they were shipping 200 packages of pure salted butter. The shipment arrived without any solicitation on the part of the defendants. On the 23rd January Messrs Schenkers & Co (shippers) telegraphed that the goods would be landed at Harwich on 26th or 27th. Following the Customs and Revenue analysis Mr Page sent samples for their own analysis and these results tallied with the Government results. Mr Page said he would be the first to stamp out any attempt at adulteration and the defendants would having nothing more to do with the butter. On the evening that they received their own results they wrote to Customs asking how they should proceed. They also telegraphed a message to the shipper: "Water in butter; illegal to sell here". The butter was ultimately sent out of the country.

To put it mildly, the present action of the Customs was 'kicking a dead horse'. Mr Page submitted that they were not importers within the meaning of the Act, and it was not a case in which the Customs needed to prosecute. The case was a trifling one and should be dismissed. The defendants did not import at Harwich and had no control there. They had no chance of refusing the goods because the letter arrived after the goods were shipped. They'd been told by the shipper that the butter was pure. Mr Ward, the HM Customs prosecutor, told the bench that the butter was valued at £960. The Chairman of the bench said the magistrates came to a unanimous decision and reluctantly found that the defendants did import the butter, which was not up to the legal standard. The bench felt that it was a case where the morally innocent had to suffer for the guilty. The defendants had done all they could when their attention was called to the poor quality. The magistrates imposed a mitigated fine of £2 and 12s costs to each of the three defendants.

I guess they were quite relieved to receive a relatively low fine, but I'm with Alfred – the case surely should not have gone to court. It seems unfair to me that 'the morally innocent had to suffer for the guilty'. What kind of fairness is that? The phrase, 'the law is an ass' comes to mind!

Three years after this court case, in January 1912, Alfred's wife Edith died at a sanatorium in Switzerland. Later that year Alfred travelled to Australia and New Zealand. I feel sure that his cousin Samuel Palgrave Page would have encouraged him to take this long trip, primarily to visit their suppliers in those countries but also to visit his brother, Thompson Scott, whom he may not have seen since he was a young boy.

There are several newspaper reports of his visit and they give an insight into the dairy business in that era. Alfred had visited several different butter factory directorates, including cooperatives. He said that Denmark had now reached the "zenith of her production", while the wealth of Germany had increased so enormously that she had not only long ceased to export butter to Great Britain, but was a large buyer from Denmark and Siberia and every year her requirements would be on a larger scale. Likewise, shipments from the United States came to an end and their vast population made increasing demands upon Canada, which had almost ceased to send butter to London and was now buying chiefly from New Zealand. It had become evident that Argentina's exports to London would not develop on the scale expected. Alfred went on,

> "There are over 45 millions of people to be fed in Great Britain, while the population of London alone is something like twice as great as you have in the whole of Australia – a country 500 square miles larger than the whole of the United States, and two-thirds the size of Europe including Russia – and every year that passes will show a great increase in population, with a proportionate decrease in the means of feeding them, except by imports and now that I have been travelling nearly five months throughout New Zealand and the Australian states and seen the enormous tracts of undeveloped country I am able to realise what I would never have known if I had remained at Home, namely, the splendid future in store for your dairying industry. I have been brought to understand the disabilities under which you have had to work, the length of time before cream reaches the factories and the long distances some of the butter has to travel before it can be shipped, so I am filled with wonder at the results which you have achieved, and I am confident that with more people working on the land and the means of communication improving each year the great success of these last 31 years will be as nothing compared with the progress of the future.

"Regarding prospects for the current season Mr Page said Great Britain had suffered from a very severe drought the summer before last, and it would be some time before any recovery in the production took place. On top of that they had exceptionally heavy rains throughout the United Kingdom, which spoilt the hay crops, the damage being estimated at £5 million. Coming so soon after the dry weather last year, this would cause a material decline in the home production. Coupled with the increased consumption, a high range of values for Australian goods was assumed. London will be more and more dependent upon Australia for supplies of dairy produce as the time goes on, and while older countries had reached their limit, this country was only just beginning. Furthermore, everything points to the fact that they will never go back to the low prices of former years."

Alfred arrived back Home during 1913 and the following year his son, Charles Carew was married to Muriel Coles, on 11th July 1914 at Capel, Surrey. Muriel was from a well-to-do family and the happy event was thoroughly reported in the local press. They must have been barely back from their honeymoon when war against Germany was declared on 4th August.

Meanwhile in Adelaide the court case moved on at snail's pace until Alfred was notified in the summer of 1917 that the land was sold, and he was entitled to his 1/18th share. Although the business had been doing very well it was probably disrupted somewhat during the war, so I guess that the Adelaide inheritance was very useful. His share was £1,222, equivalent to £72,000 in 2018. His daughter-in-law Muriel gave birth to a son, Roderic Samuel on 7th September 1917. Alfred must have been delighted with his little grandson. Charles and Muriel lived in a wonderful property, Greys, Hook Heath Road, Woking in Surrey. Alfred was still at East End House in Finchley. These were both substantial properties and both were working in the family firm with Samuel Palgrave Page. Certainly, this branch of the family had excelled financially. Interestingly, I was born in Woking, but of course no one in my family knew of this branch of the family, so no connections were made.

Sadly, this comfortable situation only lasted for four years, because on 10th April 1921 Charles died. Little Roderic was only three years old. The obituary for Charles states that he played cricket for his school, Malvern; his university, Cambridge; and also for Middlesex. He was an Association International and had captained the Cambridge team. He was 37 years old and his gross estate was valued at £6,615 (c. £390,00 in 2018 value). I have a copy of his Will, dated 8th November 1888. This was the same date that my grandfather, William Augustus Page, was Mentioned in Dispatches (MID) for gallantry in the field of war.

Charles' Will is very brief and is witnessed by two nurses, so I assume that it was written when he was injured in the war, but I have no details of his action in that conflict. However, his short Will is one of the most poignant I have read and reduces me to tears each time I read it.

> "I leave everything in my possession absolutely to the best
> wife a man ever had, Muriel Gertrude Page. To my father
> I give great thanks as being one of the best."

Just about six weeks later, on 28th May, Alfred Samuel also died. He was 65 years old. His Will was written only a week before he died. I assume this was because Charles had died and he needed Muriel to be his executrix. He left small bequests to various people involved with Holy Trinity church in Finchley, the vicar and churchwardens. He also gave £30 each to his sisters-in-law, Agnes in Australia and Clara in Suffolk. He asked Muriel to maintain the family grave at Holy Trinity. Poor Muriel had lost her husband and then her father-in-law within a couple of months and she had a young son to look after. Fortunately for her, financial security was not a problem. Alfred Samuel left estate with a net value of £15,370 (just under £1million in 2018 values).

In December 1929 Muriel married Douglas William Bingeman, a bachelor, aged 36, at St Nicholas Church Guildford. Douglas was an agent and they carried on living at Greys, Hook Heath. Roddy would have been 12 years old. No doubt he went off to boarding school; maybe Malvern, following in his father's footsteps. Ten years later and four days before his 22nd birthday war was declared against Germany and he signed up for the RAF. He was a sergeant wireless operator.

The next information I found about him was a newspaper birthday memorial: "Sgt R S Page RAFVR. In loving memory of Roddy on this his 25th birthday. He did not return from the Augsberg raid on April 17th, 1942, but died doing 'the job that had to be done'". The Augsburg Raid, also referred to as Operation Margin, was a bombing raid made by the RAF on the MAN U-boat engine plant in Augsburg, undertaken during the daylight hours of 17th April 1942. The mission was assigned to No. 44 Squadron and No. 97 Squadron, both of which were equipped with the new Avro Lancaster. Roddy is buried at Durnbach War Cemetery, Gmund am Tegernsee, Miesbacher Landkreis, Bavaria, Germany.

At this time Muriel and Douglas were living at Deolali, Hook Heath, Woking. Muriel obtained administration for Roddy's estate, which was valued at £25,708. Muriel outlived Douglas by 17 years and died in 1972, aged 80.

The family of Alfred Samuel, who had inherited a one-eighteenth share of Section 8 Goodwood, had died out.

Chapter 20

Clara Page
(spouse of first cousin three times removed)

Clara Fogg was born on 11th August 1864 in the Hammersmith area of London, where her father George was an Inspector at a water company. In the 1871 census she is living at home with her parents and several siblings. Ten years later she is a pupil at a school in Battersea. Ten years later again, in 1891 aged 26, she is listed on the census as a bookkeeper at the Albion Hotel on Marine Parade in Eastbourne.

Perhaps William Augustus Page, third son of Thompson Scott Page was on holiday one year at Eastbourne. Certainly, the Page family took holidays in that area, as Samuel Page himself had died at the Marine Hotel in Hastings in 1860. The only thing that we can do, with no family papers in existence, is to surmise about their meeting, but we know that they were married on 23rd December 1893. The ceremony was at St Stephen's Church, Hammersmith. Clara lived with her parents at 9 Wood Lane, Shepherd's Bush. Their witnesses were John Percy Sloane and Clara's older sister, Annie Margaret Fogg. William's occupation is merchant, and he was living at Penge, and that is where they made their home. He was 36 when he got married and Clara was 29.

It wasn't long before their daughter, Dora Helen, was born in September and baptised on 17th October 1894 at Christ Church Penge. They were living on Beckenham Road in Penge in the 1901 census and they employed a cook, parlour maid and housemaid.

William's occupation remains the same, provision merchant. I have no information that he was working for the family firm of Samuel Page and Son. I haven't found any records of him being admitted as a Freeman of the City of London, nor have I seen anything about his employment records nor notices of bankruptcy. It would appear that he was a provision merchant working out of 24 St John Street in the City of London. He seemed to live a normal, blameless existence. And tragically, at the age of 43 on 18th October 1901, William died.

His Will is one of the most succinct that I have ever read. It was written on 31st July 1894 and says, "This is my last Will. I give all my property to my wife whom I appoint sole executrix." The Will was signed by William Augustus Page and witnessed by J May, 24 St John Street, London EC; Witness E M Dicketts, Blendworth House, Wandsworth Common SW.

On the 1st day of March 1902 Probate of this Will, valued at £535 was granted to his wife, Clara Page, the sole executrix. Clara was widowed very young; she was 36 years old and her daughter Dora was only six. I believe that one or other of her siblings lived in Suffolk and that is where she moved to with Dora. In 1911 they were living at Brookdene, Queens Road, Felixstowe, which was quite a large house, with eight rooms. There are no servants living with them, which seems strange as ten years previously she had three live-in servants, but is probably a reflection of her straitened circumstances.

Europe was in turmoil, leading up to the first world war. Britain declared war on Germany on 4th August 1914. On the 8th October 1914 Clara's daughter Dora Helen died. She was 20 years old. The cause of death on her death certificate is disseminated sclerosis. I cannot find a specific definition that differentiates this from multiple sclerosis. Neither do I know if she had been afflicted all her short life, or if it was a recent diagnosis. It is defined as a chronic progressive nervous disorder involving loss of myelin sheath around certain nerve fibres.

My thoughts that Clara had relatives in Suffolk were confirmed when I saw who had registered Dora's death: Rosa Edith Fogg, Clara's sister, who lived on Undercliff Road, Felixstowe. In 1917 Clara came into the inheritance of her husband's 1/18 share of Section 8 Goodwood, Adelaide. It was valued at £1,222, roughly equivalent to £72,000 in 2018. She had lost her husband and their only daughter, but she could look forward to a reasonably comfortable financial future.

The next piece of information I found was Clara's death certificate. She died on the 1st of September 1924, when she was 58 years old*, at the Wembley Nursing Home Dalkeith, Ealing Road, Wembley. The cause of her death was given as encephalitis lethargica, which is defined as, "The disease attacks the brain, leaving some victims in a statue-like condition, speechless and motionless. Between 1915 and 1926, an epidemic of encephalitis lethargica spread around the world. Nearly five million people were affected, a third of whom died in the acute stages. Many of those who survived never returned to their pre-existing 'aliveness'."

Clara succumbed in 1924 and the date fits perfectly into the timeline for the epidemic. Once again Rosa Fogg was present at the death. Both sisters had evidently moved from Suffolk, into London. Rosa's address was 72 North Road, Highgate. Clara's Will was as succinct as her husbands. All her property was left to her sister, Rosa Edith Fogg, who was also sole executrix.

So, William never had the benefit of the proceeds of his grandfather's estate in Adelaide. This branch of the family had totally died out in 1924. Rosa Fogg was the recipient of Clara's estate which would have included the inheritance. Probate of Clara Page's estate of £2,573 7s 10d was granted to Rosa in October 2014. Rosa lived to the ripe old age of 88 and died in Harrow in 1964. She left £1,761.

*According to my records Clara would have been 60 when she died, but on her death certificate her age is given as 58.

Chapter 21

Samuel Palgrave Page
(first cousin three times removed)

SAMUEL PALGRAVE PAGE was the older of the two sons of Samuel Page, born in 1863 in Surbiton, Surrey. Even before their father died, Samuel and his brother Robert were wealthy young men. Their maternal uncle Robert Palgrave died in 1882 and left his entire estate between the two of them. This sum of £30,685 gave them purchasing power which would be equivalent to £2m in 2018. So, at the ages of 20 and 14 Samuel and Robert were millionaires. Their father was the trustee until they came of age.

Their father died in 1890 and he left £47,668, mostly to his sons, in addition to his paintings. At the ripe ages of 28 and 22 the sons came into an inheritance which has an approximate value of £2m each in 2018. Despite all this wealth it doesn't seem that they went off the rails, or sat back in the lap of luxury. They were both inculcated by their father with the Protestant work ethic. Samuel was educated at Bradfield School in Berkshire.

We already have seen that Samuel Palgrave Page took on the case of trying to establish Martha Page's share of Section 8 Goodwood in Adelaide in 1892, and to then purchase it from her, so that she had some funds. My assumption is that Samuel Palgrave was a kindly man, like his father, and knowing how fortunate he was financially, probably felt that he could expend his energy and expertise in helping Martha to obtain her rightful inheritance. In addition to inheriting the 1/12th share of Section 8,

Samuel had purchased Martha's 1/6th share. He now owned one quarter of Goodwood Section 8.

After finishing at school, Samuel Palgrave Page worked in the family business, Samuel Page and Son, based at 16 Water Lane, Tower Street, City of London. He married Mary Harris on 15th June 1887 at Holy Trinity, Westbury on Trym, Gloucestershire. Mary's father Samuel was a schoolmaster and a visiting lecturer at Reading University and was a witness at their wedding, as was Samuel Page. Three Samuels at one wedding – fortunately, when their one and only son was born, on 29th March 1890, they called him Horace Palgrave Page. It might be that Samuel met Mary when he was at school at Bradfield, as Samuel Harris was a schoolmaster and lived in that area. Samuel and Mary initially lived at 'Oakleigh' in Surbiton. In 1891 they had three servants and Samuel's brother Robert was living with them and their baby son.

Frederick Layton, the American meat-packer, to whose gallery in Milwaukee Samuel Page the Younger donated a painting, outlived Samuel. In 1892 he made one of his frequent visits to London, both for business and pleasure, accompanied by his wife and their niece Grace Hayman. Grace's diary entry for 22nd June 1892 is interesting.

> "We started out about 10 o'clock, went first to the French Gallery to see Uncle's bust. Saw a very fine picture; before leaving Uncle bought it. Also saw the piece of sculpture Music and Art. From there went to the Dudley Gallery. The day was very warm. We lunched at the hotel then drove down to the City near London Bridge. Uncle went in to see Mr Page. On our way back went into St Paul's. To the Empire in the evening – Versailles – grand ballet."

It is good to know that the business connections made by Samuel Page the Younger, carried on with his son and nephew running the business.

During the next ten years Samuel and Mary moved up in the world. They purchased Mottingham Hall in Mottingham, Eltham

Kent. It was about eight miles from the centre of London, so easily commutable. I assume that being south of the river encouraged the relocation of the business offices to Montague Chambers, situated next to Southwark Cathedral. I found a brief account of Mottingham Hall on a Bromley website:

> "It was situated on Mottingham Lane, set in 4 acres of ground extending to the Grove Park Hospital and bounded by the River Quaggy. Originally it was owned by James Moore (1838) and was situated on Fairy Hill. In its latter years Mottingham Hall was occupied by Sir Samuel Palgrave Page, probably until 1920, but the house may not have been the original building. His name figures prominently in Parish Council minutes as Chairman for a number of years; on the occasion of Queen Victoria's Diamond Jubilee (1897) he opened the grounds of Mottingham Hall for the children to enjoy sports there."

Samuel Palgrave Page was never knighted, so the 'Sir' information is incorrect. One other interesting piece of information is that W G Grace, the eminent cricketer is recorded as living at 'Fairhurst', Mottingham Lane in the 1911 census, which was next door to Mottingham Hall.

In 1911 Samuel and Mary are still at Mottingham Hall, which had twenty rooms. With Horace away at school they must have rattled around. They had five servants: a cook, two parlour maids and two housemaids. There was also Mottingham Lodge, a four-roomed house in which resided Albert Harrison, their coachman, with his wife and four daughters. Horace was at boarding school in Folkestone.

As one of the principal London dealers in Queensland butter, Samuel contributed to the Parliamentary Committee in 1906 that was preparing the materials for Lord Carrington's Butter Adulteration Bill. He said that faking would not be effectively stopped until those who engaged in it were liable to prison. "So strongly" he said, "do I feel about it that if a man offended twice I would give a magistrate the option of sending him to prison, and for a third offence there should be imprisonment without the option of a fine".

Samuel was a JP, in addition to being Chairman of the Parish Council. He was also busy with other appointments. I read in his Will that he had been President of the British Dairy Farmer's Association. He left them his portrait which had been painted by Edward Parry. This caused me some excitement, having always lamented that all the family portraits passed down from Samuel Page had just 'disappeared'. I contacted the archivist of what is now the Royal Association of British Dairy Farmers at Stoneleigh. She was amused when I asked whether they still had the portrait. They had moved out of London, years before, and she felt sure that all old portraits would have been filed 'skip'. How very disappointing. So near and yet so far.

A couple of days later she contacted me. Joy of joys! She had looked through their year books and had found references to Samuel Palgrave Page in 1913 and 1937 which contained his picture. In 1913 he was President of the organisation. The 1937 entry is his obituary. She very kindly emailed the scanned pages to me. They are laudatory about S P Page and I think it would be a shame to paraphrase them, so I reproduce them here in full.

Mr S Palgrave Page – President 1913

For many years Mr Page has taken the keenest interest in the work of the Association, his sole aim being always to advance its influence in dairying generally, so that much of the popularity it now enjoys may be attributed to his persistent efforts. As chairman of the Finance and General Purposes Committee, Mr Page's work for the British Dairy Farmers' Association has been untiring and ever increasing, so that the present solid financial position of the Association is mainly due to his practical judgment and guidance.

Perhaps it may not be commonly known that Mr S Palgrave Page is senior partner in a well-known firm of produce brokers in the City of London, and consequently he is always in close touch with matters pertaining to dairy produce. Naturally, his advice and commercial capabilities have therefore been of the greatest service to the Council. Those members who attended the Conference in Ireland last summer can testify to the wonderful organisation and precision with which every detail was carried out under his guidance.

Mr Page cannot perhaps be classified as a dairy farmer pure and simple in the accepted sense of the term, but he keeps a small herd of choice Jersey cattle at his residence, Mottingham Hall, besides a loft of Dragoon pigeons, of which he was at one time a large and very successful exhibitor. He has been four times President of the National Peristeronic Society, one of the oldest Columbarian Societies, and was one of the founders of the Dragoon Clun, which annually gives several of its gold medals for competition at the Dairy Show. He is also a Liveryman of one of the oldest City Companies, viz, the Goldsmiths.

With the expiration of Mr Page's Presidentship the lease of the present office of the Association in Hanover Square terminated; and mainly due to his efforts more extensive and spacious premises in Russell Square were acquired, where it is the hope of the Council that the guiding influence and practical knowledge of S Palgrave Page may be as keenly evident as they have been during so many years past.

Memoir of the Late Samuel Palgrave Page, JP (1937)

Through his death, the British Dairy Farmers' Association has lost one of its most valuable members and his sound advice and untiring efforts at all times will be sadly missed, more especially by his colleagues on the Council with whom he laboured for so many years.

Mr Page, who joined the Association on 6th June 1886, took such a keen interest in its many activities that in 1890 he was elected to a seat on the Council. From 1892 until 1907 he acted as a Press Steward at the Dairy Show, and for many years from 1903 was a Steward of Refreshments. For a considerable period, he was Chairman of the Reception Committee and the many duties he was called upon to perform were always carried out in a most admirable and efficient manner.

In 1907 he was elected Chairman of the Finance and General Purposes Committee, a position he continually held until he resigned in 1921, and from 1899 until 1923 he acted as Chairman of the Poultry and Pigeon Committee. In addition, he acted on many Sub-Committees, and in view of his thorough knowledge of the Association's activities and considered opinions, his advice was invariably sought on matters requiring thoughtful consideration.

Palgrave Page, on leaving Bradfield, started his career in his father's firm of Samuel Page & Son, at that time in Water Lane, Tower Street, removing in later years to Montague Chambers, London Bridge. The firm, which was established in 1805, acted as agents on commission for the sale of Australian and New Zealand Butter, cheese, bacon and eggs, with similar interests in Canada as well as the continent of Europe and the United States of America. Apart from his business interests, his chief interest in life seemed to be wrapped up in the fortunes and the success of the Association, to which he devoted so great a part of his time and thought, and his regular attendance at the various council and committee meetings makes his loss the more keenly felt. In his early days he was a keen and successful pigeon fancier and his long association with the Poultry and Pigeon Committee was ever of the greatest help. From its earliest days he was Chairman of the Pigeon Marking Conference and, when the National Pigeon Association came into existence about 1917 Mr Page became its first President and remained in that office until the annual meeting last year when, through ill-health, he felt compelled to resign.

A Society also whose interests he always had very much at heart was the National Peristeronic Society, founded as far back as 1847, and the oldest pigeon club in existence. He joined it in 1883 and remained a subscribing member to the end. For some years he acted as its Honorary Secretary and on four occasions was its President.

Mr Page was held in very high esteem by the Association's clerical staff, and it was he who engaged our present Secretary as a junior clerk in 1909.

An announcement in *The London Gazette* of 21st March 1930 indicates that Samuel Palgrave Page has retired from business:

Notice is hereby given that the Partnership heretofore subsisting between Samuel Palgrave Page and Charles Joseph Pollard carrying on business, as Provision Agents, at Montague Chambers, London Bridge, Southwark, in the county of Surrey, under the style or firm of SAMUEL PAGE & SON, has been dissolved by mutual consent s from the first day of January, one thousand nine hundred and thirty, so far as concerns the said Samuel Palgrave Page, who retires from the said firm. All debts due to and owing by the said late firm will be received and paid by the said Charles Joseph Pollard, who will continue the said business under the present style or firm of Samuel Page & Son – dated this 19th day of March 1930.

So, with the death of his cousin Alfred Samuel Page in 1921 and his own retirement in 1930 the name of Page remained in the title of the firm only. No 'Pages' now worked for Samuel Page & Co.

Charles Pollard carried on the business for some years. It had become a subsidiary of Dalgety's the shipping company in 1910, which continued until the breakup of Dalgety's in 1998. Samuel Page & Co had been in existence from 1805 for 193 years. Extraordinarily none of my immediate Page relatives knew of the existence of this business of their distant cousins.

Back to Samuel Palgrave Page. After his retirement, he and Mary, together with Horace, moved to a mansion flat in London, 27 Oakwood Court, Kensington. Horace was a Lieutenant and then a Major in the Prince of Wales Regiment in the first world war. However, there are no service records for him, apart from a medal request in 1923, giving his address as Oakwood Court.

On the 15th June 1937 there was a brief announcement in the press that Samuel and Mary had been married for 50 years. Samuel only just made his Golden Wedding Anniversary as less than two months later he died, on 4th August.

As one would expect, his Will is full of interesting items. In the absence of other family documentation, and aside from birth, marriage and death registrations, Wills are the best source of information. Samuel left his erstwhile business partner Charles Pollard a piece of plate or an oil painting or water colour, "as a memento of the pleasant personal and business relations that existed between us".

His portrait by Edward Parry was donated to the British Diary Farmers Association after his wife's death. He also desired that his son should have a small replica of it.

He left the family portraits to his brother Robert, "so that their ultimate disposal may rest with the survivor of us":

Thompson Scott – founder of the firm of Samuel Page & Son

Samuel Page the Elder

Mrs Samuel Page the Elder

Samuel Page the Younger

Mrs Samuel Page the Younger

And the following small portraits

Mrs Samuel Page the Younger

Mrs Robert Palgrave

Her grandfather Thomas

He left Mary's sister Phoebe £50 and his cousin Alice Platt (née Blenkarn) £20. There were various similar bequests to friends.

When he left Mottingham Hall in 1920 most of his staff were taken over by the Metropolitan and Asylums board. A man called Harry Hearnden's services had been dispensed with by the board and Samuel had given him various sums from time to time when he was short of employment. Samuel desired that Harry should be further helped in this manner or given a weekly allowance of 10 shillings if he became unable to work. To previous employees of Samuel Page & Son (whether or not still in their employ) he left

F W Moore £35, A Hitch £23, P C Crowe £16, C Clark £16, and Miss S Solomon (Typist) £5.

He left all his real and personal estate to his wife, Mary, together with £500 immediately. It seemed strange that he didn't make provision for Horace. Instead he asked Mary "to make such provision for our son Horace Palgrave Page during her lifetime as she may find convenient and to bequeath capital to him by Will and/or set up a trust for him", and that she should "consult the Executors of my Will and be guided by their advice".

To his brother Robert he left "any two oil paintings or water colours that he may select and the silver Cigar Box presented to me by the residents of Mottingham in 1912 as I believe he will atttach greater value to these articles as a token of my affection than that of a pecuniary legacy".

He asks his relatives to maintain the upkeep of the two family graves at Norwood Cemetery and one in Kensal Green Cemetery and that of his old nurse Jane Trott in Grove Park Cemetery. And then come his final personal wishes:

> "I desire that no mourning shall be worn for me and that my funeral be announced in the obituary column of *The Times* as Private to indicate that I should prefer it to be attended only by such near relations and friends as may survive me but not excluding anyone who for special reasons may wish to do so, also that an artery of my body be opened as proof that death has taken place and that a qualified Medical man be paid an appropriate fee for that purpose."

Oh my! I've heard that Victorians asked for a little bell be attached to their fingers so that they could ring for help if they were buried prior to actual death. But having an artery opened is a little macabre, but I guess it is indicative of Samuel's attention to the smallest detail. His last paragraph is not much more savoury:

> "Lastly, I desire that my body be burned and the ashes buried in my parents' grave in the South Metropolitan Cemetery, West Norwood, where there is room for us all."

The net value of his estate was £17,570.

Mary stayed on at Oakwood Court for a little while until she and Horace moved out to the West Country. In the 1939 census they are both listed as living on private means, at the Phillips Court Annexe, Livermead Cliff Hotel, Torquay. Also staying there was Susan Lengerke, a partly retired trained nurse. Susan Lengerke lived with, or near, them when they moved to Cheltenham. Mary died on the 3rd May 1945, just a few days before VE day (Victory in Europe) on 8th May, at Glenmore, The Park, Cheltenham in Gloucestershire.

In her Will, Mary left £17,615. Susan Lengerke received £500. From the Trust Fund Miss E Hearnden (sister of Harry Hearnden) would receive £20 per annum, for life. The Trustees were also tasked with providing an income for Horace from the Trust Fund. I was puzzled that Horace wasn't left money from his father, or his mother. Something odd was going on. He had been in the army in the first world war. I wondered if he had suffered shell shock or some other psychiatric illness. He seemed always to have lived with his parents according to censuses. There was no indication of any employment, in fact scarcely any information about him at all.

As is usual with most wills, Mary's goes on at length about leaving the Trust funds to children, children's spouses and issue. But Horace had no wife or issue. And if this was the case, then on his death, the Trust funds would go to her various brothers and sisters: Lucy Holman, Biddy Vine Stevens, Tom Harris, Sam and Dorothy Harris, Molly Blyth, Flossie Sly, Edith Thorne and sister-in-law Phoebe Harris. Lucky Flossie also received her squirrel coat. Horace was to receive all her furniture and household articles, apart from her sofa table with drop ends, which was for Susan Lengerke. Her two maids Frances Sykes and Kathleen Lidbetter were to receive one year's wages.

Mary was 85 when she passed away. Less than a month later, on 31st May 1945, her son Horace Palgrave Page also died. The cause of death was cerebral haemorrhage and cirrhosis of the liver.

Susan Lengerke registered the death. A post-mortem, without inquest, took place. A post-mortem is usually carried out if the death is unexpected. The fact that there wasn't an inquest would indicate that there was nothing suspicious about the death. As already mentioned, Horace was a shadowy figure, and he left no Will, so nothing is known about him. He was 55 years old, and with him the family nearly died out. However, there was still his uncle Robert Palgrave Page and we'll meet him in the next chapter.

Chapter 22

Robert Palgrave Page
(first cousin three times removed)

SAMUEL'S YOUNGER BROTHER Robert was only six years old when his mother died in 1873. In addition to his aunt Adelaide, who was living with them at the time, he had Jane Trott as a nurse, and the household was not short of servants. He went to prep school, St Michael's near Eton when he was 11, and then went on to Harrow when he was 13 or 14. Harrow was, and is, a superb public school, the very best. After Harrow he entered Trinity Hall at Cambridge University, again one of the very best educational establishments. He graduated with a BA in 1890 and was admitted to the Inner Temple, one of the Inns of Court, on 22nd March 1887. He may have been a barrister but there aren't any records of him in that profession.

He was a great traveller and there is something a little 'shady' about his existence. He may have worked for the Foreign Office or the Secret Service, but it is difficult to establish facts between his arrival at the Inns of Court and the first world war – that is 27 years of not knowing quite what he was doing! He lived initially at 62 Carlisle Mansions, then moved to number 73. In the 1920s and 1930s he resided at 33 Dover Street, in the heart of Mayfair. He had nothing to do with the firm Samuel Page and Son.

However, come the first world war there is a little more information. He was made a Member of the British Empire (MBE) in 1917. He was a civil assistant to the Intelligence Directorate in the War Office. Also in 1917, in common with his brother and cousins he received his Goodwood Section 8 inheritance. His share was 1/12 of the proceeds of the sale, which was approximately £1,833.

Almost 100 years later, in October 2014, Bonhams, the Auction House, offered a lot entitled 'War Scraps collected by R P Page CBE, Intelligence Directorate War Office 1914-19'. It was Lot 38 and sold for just over £1,000. It was described as a 60-page book with 13 autograph or typed letters signed by Lloyd George, Dunnington-Jefferson and others to Page. Also, pictorial Christmas cards and 13 other ephemera relating to the Intelligence Services.

The description continues: An album relating to the experiences of Robert P Page of MO5 (MI5) and his relations with the Intelligence Corps from 1915-1919. His typescript narrative interspersed with letters and printed ephemera; the Chief Field Censor BEF (5/7/1915) writes that "... thanks in considerable measure to the excellent men you have sent us lately I think the censorship is more efficient now than it ever has been". A Pass issued from GHQ to Page to allow him to visit France "on military duty" (August 1915) beside his account of the journey to interview and assess candidates for "internships in Turkish" (2 out of 16 possibles were selected); caricature Christmas cards from the Intelligence Section, signed by Dunnington-Jefferson (Commandant of the Corps "... the liaison between your office and mine has worked admirably"); Arthur A Fenn and others; a letter from Prime Minister Lloyd George informing Page of his being made an MBE; descriptions of visits to the Continent in the last months and following year of the war, with comments on the scope of the Intelligence Corps activities.

Visiting Cologne in 1919 he records that 'men are employed in listening on all telephone lines, principally trunk lines into unoccupied territory and obtain much information as to the Bolshevik machinations and evasions of our regulations ....', and

'Captain Craig would have no hesitation in employing German officials more extensively on our behalf, so entirely have they acquired the habit of obedience', before inspecting the rooms to be used by the Women Censors '…what was the ballroom, all very comfortable with central heating'. Whilst in Dunkirk he notes that the British Army has been busy 'catching some of the Chinese who are living as highwaymen in the devastated area. The leader of the gang …was a General of the Southern Army, who when things became too hot for him in China enlisted in our Labour Battalions (Chinese Labour Corps)'.

What a find online! I wrote to Bonhams asking if they had more information on who had sold or bought it. The information was confidential, but they did write to the buyer. He telephoned me. He was a very old and infirm gentleman, living in Dorset. I did not even catch his name as after a brief conversation he handed me to his carer to finish the call. He had an interest in the Army, which is why he purchased the document. He did tell me that he'd let the War Museum have sight of it for copying for their archives. However, when I called the War Museum, they told me that they did not archive this sort of information. So, sadly I will never see it, but the auction house description does give a reasonable insight into Robert's occupation during WW1.

On his retirement in May 1919 Mansfield Cumming, first chief of SIS (MI6) wrote sending him a cigarette box to be engraved by Mappin and Webb. I did know a little bit about this item. Jumping on a few years to Robert's Will, he left the silver cigarette box to his goddaughter Joan Alison Fenn, daughter of his friend Lieutenant-Colonel A A Fenn DSO, late Commanding Officer 1st Battalion Sherwood Foresters. In addition, she received £2,000. It states that the box was presented to him by the Chief of the Secret Service and inscribed in the lid "From a grateful Department for valuable help 1914-1919".

Of the two best known family history websites one gives information about travel by ship from the UK and the other gives details of travel to the UK. Neither of them has full information, but there are several entries for Robert. He always travelled first class and his occupation is listed as 'gentleman' or 'none'. He had plenty of money so may have been travelling to explore the world, or he may, as suggested, have been in the employ of the secret service.

1903: arrived in New York, from San Juan, Puerto Rico.

1909: travelled from Liverpool to Quebec, Canada

1909: crossed the Canadian border to the US at Vancouver

1920: sailed to Bombay from London

1924: in Plymouth from Bombay, via Aden, Suez and Port Said

1926: from Havana, Cuba to Miami then New York to Southampton

1930: from Brisbane to London, via Sydney, Port Said and Gibraltar. On this voyage he is 62 years of age and gives his occupation as retired Army Officer.

Robert's entry in 'Who's Who' gives one of his interests as foreign travel and his club as The Travellers, which is hardly surprising. It was a club founded in 1819, 'for gentlemen who had travelled out of the British Isles to a distance of at least five hundred miles from London in a direct line'. Membership was extended to foreign visitors and diplomats posted to London. It was first housed at 12 Waterloo Place but soon outgrew the space, moving to 49 Pall Mall. In 1826 money was raised to lease part of the grounds of Carlton House and Charles Barry, who later designed the Reform Club next door and the Houses of Parliament, was appointed as architect.

The original concept of The Travellers Club by Lord Castlereagh and others dates from the return of peace in Europe following the Napoleonic Wars. They envisaged a club where gentlemen who travelled abroad might meet and offer hospitality to distinguished foreign visitors. Arrangements for the establishment of The Travellers Club were finalised at a meeting in the spring of 1819, attended by distinguished diplomats, travellers and two future

Prime Ministers, the Earl of Aberdeen and Viscount Palmerston. The head of Ulysses was adopted as the Club symbol.

Throughout the Club's existence, distinguished members of the Diplomatic Service, the Home Civil Service, and the Armed Forces have come to the Travellers Club, while other professions have increasingly been added to the membership, as international travel has become part of the working life of a wider and wider range of occupations. The Club currently maintains reciprocal arrangements with some 140 clubs across the world.

Robert was appointed CBE in 1920, so his war work had certainly been recognised. In addition to his travelling he listed his interests in 'Who's Who' as fishing and shooting. I haven't discovered any evidence of his shooting interest but there is plenty of fishing information. He belonged to the Houghton Fishing Club, based at the Grosvenor Hotel, Stockbridge in Hampshire. Robert edited a book entitled "Further Chronicles of the Houghton Fishing Club, 1908-1932". It was a limited edition print of 350 copies, and antiquarian book sellers offer it these days for over £250.

The Houghton Fishing Club is a small, select group of fly fishermen. I called into the Grosvenor Hotel one afternoon in the hope of obtaining some information, but none was forthcoming. When a club is so secretive it is likely that facts become confused with rumour, but I have tried to record only accurate information. *Country Life* ran an article on 'clubs that you cannot join' in 2008, which states that The Houghton Fishing Club has exclusive fishing rights on 13 miles of the River Test, near Stockbridge in Hampshire. The HFC is famously very private and has a restricted elected membership of 25. Lord Tanlaw, Lord Tryon and the Duke of Northumberland are members. In 2010 the following article appeared in *The Independent* newspaper.

> "Famous for its gin-clear waters and manicured banks, the river Test in Hampshire is one of the world's most impressive fishing spots, a favourite of presidents and prime

ministers – and of a certain combative television inter-
viewer. The reason: copious brown trout.

"But this autumn the river where Jeremy Paxman is fond of
casting a line has been discoloured by pollution, angering
members of the exclusive fishing club that enjoys rights to
fish there and threatening the livelihood of local businesses
that rely on famous visitors' passing trade.

"The Test is home to the Houghton club, founded in 1822,
where a quarter of members are lords and knights. Among
those who have taken their rods to this exclusive stretch of
water – the 11 miles of banks are valued at £600 a foot –
are Jimmy Carter, George Bush Snr and Prince Charles, as
well as other highly recognisable anglers such as Eric
Clapton, Vinnie Jones, Ian Botham and Marco Pierre White."

It hasn't been possible to find out who might have been
members in Robert's day, but no doubt he was in some very good
company. He evidently found the Grosvenor Hotel to his liking,
because with the dark clouds of war looming, he moved west
away from the capital, like his sister-in-law and nephew, just
before WW2 started. The Grosvenor Hotel was given as his
address on his Will.

In his Will he left the Committee of the Houghton Fishing Club
£1,300 to be used to cancel his shares in the club on his death. He
left all his rods and other fishing tackle to Mr T Murray Sowerby
of Blackwell Down, Flax Bourton near Bristol, suggesting that he
might put them at the disposal of any club members who might
like to use them.

As well as the silver cigarette box bequeathed to his goddaughter Alison, Robert left his nephew Horace the silver cigar box given
by the residents of Mottingham to his brother in 1912. He also left
his nephew all the family portraits. The same ones that were listed
in the chapter on Samuel Palgrave Page. Robert had another
goddaughter, Anne Bell, the daughter of Lieutenant-Colonel
Gilbert H Keighley MC, who had been Commanding Officer of
the 1st Battalion South Lancashire Regiment. To Anne he left

£1,000. As mementoes of long-established friendship, he left £200 each to Arthur H Hoare of Fleet Street and Lieutenant Colonel H W Holland of Camberley.

He then goes on to give instructions for the family graves. He donated £325 to Kensal Green cemetery for the upkeep of graves, 20188, 22151 and 28160 which were the graves of family members of his uncle Robert Palgrave. To the South Metropolitan cemetery at West Norwood he left £347 to maintain the graves 5799 of Samuel Page the Elder and 9377 of Samuel Page the Younger, the latter grave being where he desired to be buried. He asked that the gravestones be kept in good repair with the inscriptions clear and legible and that the graves be planted with spring and summer flowers.

He appointed his Trustees and Executors, James Ashurst le Brasseur and Meadows Martineau, solicitors of Carey Street, Lincolns Inn, City of London to pay the income from his invested estate to his nephew Horace Palgrave Page. After his nephew's death, or if he should predecease Robert then the residuary estate income should be applied to the King Edward's Hospital Funds for London, whose offices were at Old Jewry in the City of London.

He then directs that if he should die at Stockbridge or other country district during the War his body should be cremated, and his ashes then taken at a convenient time to be buried in the family grave 9377 at Norwood Cemetery. He desired that there should be no mourning and no flowers at his funeral.

His Will was written in 1942. As noted in the last chapter his nephew, Horace, died in May 1945. Robert therefore added a codicil to his Will in 1946, which states that he had bequeathed the income from his residuary estate to his nephew, but as he had died, he declared the following,

> "My Trustees shall stand possessed of my said residuary estate to pay the income thereof to Mrs Susan Lengerke of 15 Hay Street, Marshfield near Chippenham, during her life in greater gratitude for the good services she has rendered

to the members of my late brothers family for so many years".

Robert died on the 30th April 1947 at The Nursing Home, Sarum Road, Winchester. The gross value of his estate was £79,009, and death duty taxes of £23,775 were paid to the Inland Revenue. Robert did not marry, had no children, so his estate went out of the family. The purchasing power equivalent in 2018 would be £2,800,000.

Chapter 23

Arthur Claud Page
(my great-great uncle)

THE FIRST TIME I came across Arthur was on my grandparent's wedding certificate. He was one of the witnesses at their marriage in Standen, Hertfordshire on 7th January 1917. My grandfather, William Augustus Page, Squadron Quarter Master Sergeant, King Edwards Horse, had 10 days leave from the battlefields of northern France. Having been engaged for some time to Florence Emily Spencer they used that precious leave to marry and to honeymoon in London.

Seeing the signature of A C Page set me wondering 'who was this Page relative?' Recalling that my grandfather was an orphan and I only knew of his maternal grandfather, Robert Denny Briggs and his Uncle Harry Briggs. Now my task was to research A C Page. I was pleased that my orphaned grandfather did have some Page relatives and was close enough to them that Arthur acted as his best man.

It transpired that Arthur Claud was born on 23rd August 1880 in Cricklewood. He was the youngest child of William Augustus and Frances Page. He was the much younger brother of my great-grandfather William Augustus Page, who died in Quetta in 1888. Arthur was therefore only eight when his brother died. William went out to Malta with the Army in 1885, or possibly earlier, so Arthur would not have remembered this brother who was 19 years his senior.

When Arthur's father died in 1896, Arthur was only 16 and continued living at home with his mother, Frances and his older sister Edith. Edith, as we have seen, left her husband in Philadelphia and took up residence with her mother until the end of her days.

The *Evening Standard* of 12th July 1900 reported that several members of the 19th Middlesex Regiment were summoned for payment of 38 shillings, being the equivalent of the per capita grant, which the Regiment had lost because these men had failed to pass the annual 'efficiency test' of attendance and proficiency in military skills. Arthur Claude was one of them. His defence was that when he joined the 19th Middlesex he was living close to the headquarters, but business had since taken him to Putney. He did not leave work until between 7 and 8 o'clock and it was impossible for him to attend drill at the HQ of the 19th Middlesex. He'd applied to be transferred to another local unit as he was anxious to remain in the Volunteers and do his duty like a man. The reply he received was to the effect that he would receive his discharge on paying 45 shillings.

In 1901 Arthur was 20 years old and living at 15 Borneo Street in Wandsworth with his mother who is living on her own means and Edith who is recorded at 'lady's companion'. Arthur was the manager of a blind manufacturer. Discovering these details prompted some old memories of my younger days. My mother remembered her mother-in-law mentioning that there were some relatives who lived in Surbiton and had a business making blinds. The blinds were not the type for domestic interiors. Not so much in evidence these days, the blinds were made from heavy canvas and were used by shopkeepers to protect their perishable goods from the sun in summer. They might be plain, with the shop name printed on them, or could be colourfully striped. I remember the fishmonger in the town where I grew up having such a blind. He had a long pole with a hook on the end with which he pulled the blind down when necessary. My mother's memory never extended to naming these relatives, but they were certainly assumed to be Pages. Now I was discovering just who they were.

Ten years later, in 1911, Arthur was 30 and Frances and Edith were still living with him. They had moved to 10 Victoria Avenue, Surbiton which was an eight-roomed house. Living with them was Alice Pearce an 18-year-old general domestic servant. Another occupant was an eight-year-old boy, Arthur Harry Page, Arthur's nephew, who had been born in Piccadilly, London. Researching family history can be like peeling back the layers of an onion, there is always another one underneath. A Russian doll could be another analogy. You hope that something will be inside the big outer doll, but you don't know whether it will be empty or whether it will contain another ten dolls. I thought that I had quite a handle on most of the grandchildren of Frances and William. However, their eldest son, Harry Ernest, was an enigma. He was a nurseryman working in Hampstead in his youth but then had become a valet working in the St James area of London. I eventually deduced that the young Arthur was the son of Harry Ernest, as he'd been born in central London. When I found Harry on the 1911 census he was living in Dorset. His wife was Mary, or May, Rose. Harry was living at 3 Trinity Street, Dorchester, where he was the valet and Mary the working housekeeper to Major Charles Cumberland, a retired Army officer. On the census return it states that they had two children. I have not been able to track down their marriage certificate nor birth certificates for their children, nor have I been able to track down the second child.

Coming back to Arthur, we know that in 1917 he was at my grandfather's wedding and that later that year he inherited his share of Goodwood Section 8. Both he and his cousin, Rose Blenkarn, were the youngest children in their families, just like their Aunt Adelaide. They also took care of their parents, as was quite common and even expected of the youngest child. I feel sure that this was the reason that Adelaide selected this niece and nephew to inherit her Adelaide shares. Arthur's share was 1/6th, the same as Rose and it would have had a purchasing power equivalent in 2018 to just over a quarter of a million pounds. And the residual estate of Aunt Adelaide was also shared between them. Arthur was in the very fortunate position of being able to support both his mother and sister. There is no record of when the monies of the sale of Section 8 Goodwood were paid out to the recipients, but possibly it would have been late in 1917 or early 1918. Of course, WW1 was still raging until November 1918 and Frances would have been concerned for the safety of her grand-sons who were in the services. She did not see the end of the war, as she died in March 1918.

Arthur was eight years older than his nephew William Augustus Page, a.k.a. Bill, and would have been 36 when Bill married my grandmother. Whether it was his inheritance, or the death of his mother, that spurred Arthur on to marriage is not known, but on 24th April 1918 he married Elsie Taylor at the Parish Church, New Malden and Coombe, Surrey. His occupation is interesting. It says that he is a Government Contractor and a Captain of the 5th Battalion Surrey Volunteer Regiment. This unit was for home defence, for those who were over the serving age for the regular army.

They set up home at 'Ivydene', Southborough Road, Surbiton and bought a seaside retreat, a bungalow named 'Petonia', at Bracklesham Bay near Chichester, Sussex. Their son Peter Francis was born during the last quarter of 1919. This boy would have been about nine months older than my father, but I never heard him mention this cousin. Peter would actually have been my grandfather's cousin, and thus first-cousin-once-removed to my father. In due course a second son, Anthony Lawrence, arrived in June 1923.

The 1911 census is the last one that can be seen online. The 1921 census will become available in 2021. I had found, unless the family member is up before the courts or is a worthy citizen mentioned in the press, it is difficult to find out any interesting information.

I obtained Arthur's Will, which contained one or two nuggets of gold. There was the name of his Blind Manufacturing company: the Artistic Blind Company. I began to research that company in the Surrey area pre-war. That was unsuccessful, but I noticed that there was currently a company named The Artistic Blind Company in the Bristol area. I received a response to my email asking for information of their history and whether they were connected to Arthur Page. My respondee, John, sent me his version of events. He had joined Deans Blinds in Putney as a salesman in 1954. His understanding was that Peter Page had left Deans (who were the national blind company) pre-WW2 to found the Artistic Blind Company in Surbiton. In 1962, John was promoted to Sales Manager and the man he replaced moved to be the MD of The Artistic Blind Company, now owned by Waites, contractors of Wallington. In the mid-70s after various moves within the world of blinds John started his own company. He needed a name for it and, as he said, "what better than the Artistic Blind Company, (ABC)". He checked that the name was no longer in use; it wasn't, so he registered it as his company.

I believe that John's recollection that Peter Page started the Artistic Blind Company pre-war is actually not Peter, but Arthur. The fact that in the 1901 census Arthur is a manager of a blind maker and in 1911 is an employer of men indicates that he started his own company. And why not? He certainly had plenty of financial capital. I was pleased to get just a little bit more information that seemed relevant to Arthur's business.

Arthur died on 14th April 1942 and his Will gives much information about the man. He appointed Elsie, his son Peter, and his business manager of the Artistic Blind Company, Percival Clarence Hewson to be the Trustees and Executors of his Will.

He left Elsie his diamond pin and £200, as well as Ivydene and Petonia. There were copious instructions as to keeping the properties taxed and insured. The income from Arthur's Trust Fund was to be paid to Elsie during her lifetime. However, if she married again, or on her death the income would go to his two sons in equal shares. She also received all the household and garden furniture and effects.

For Peter there was a silver presentation cigarette box, his crocodile cigar case, his mahogany desk and his Founder Member Jewel. Anthony received his wristlet presentation watch and silver cigarette case and his Rotary Club Past President's Badge. To his manager, Percival Clarence Hewson he bequeathed his oak roll top desk, his Royal Warrant Holders Medal and £150. The only bequest to a non-immediate family member was his plain gold ring to his sister Kathleen Octavia Bond (née Page). If Harry Coxhead was still in his employ at the date of his death, he was to receive £50.

His bequests for allocation of his shares and debentures in the company are a little bit more complicated. Four hundred shares were to form the basis of the Trust from which to pay an income to Elsie in her lifetime, or until she married again, at which point the income would be for Peter and Anthony in equal shares when they had reached the aged of 21. Another 400 shares were on Trust for his son Peter, absolutely. One hundred and ninety shares were on Trust for Anthony on his attaining the age of 21.

He requested that his body be cremated at the Woking Crematorium. This was the first crematorium in the UK, founded in 1878 by Sir Henry Thompson, surgeon and physician to Queen Victoria. Woking's other claim to fame, other than that I was born there, is that the first purpose-built mosque in the UK, the Shah Jahan Mosque, was opened there in 1889.

Arthur asked that his friends and relatives should send no flowers to his funeral but if they desired to pay any tribute to his memory, they should send donations to the "Charley Box" fund of the Kingston-upon-Thames Rotary Club. Finally, he requested that his ashes be scattered in the garden of the crematorium in the same place as those of his sister Edith Gill, who had died in 1933.

His death was reported in the *Surrey Advertiser* on the 18th April:

> "Mr Arthur Claud Page of Ivydene, Southborough Road, Surbiton, who died on Tuesday was a founder and managing director of the Artistic Blind Company, Surbiton and former member of the Surbiton Council and in 1925-6 President of the Kingston Rotary Club. In recent years he has been a cripple. He leaves a widow and two sons."

Arthur died in the middle of WW2. The Probate certificate states that Peter Francis Page is a Lieutenant in the British Army. I haven't been able to find out very much about Peter. There are so many Peter Pages – more than 700 entries in Ancestry.com for the military alone. There are also marriages for four Peter Francis Pages in the Kingston area with dates that could be possible. I cannot verify any of them because they are just listings, not the full marriage certificate which is available online for London marriages. So, I have drawn a blank with him. If he married and had children, they are likely to still be around. Perhaps one of them will read this book and contact me. That would be marvellous.

I have more information about Anthony Lawrence, but it is not joyous. Anthony was a 2nd Lieutenant in The Royal Fusiliers (City of London Regiment) attached to The Nigeria Regiment, Royal West Africa Frontier Force (RWAFF). He was killed in action on 15th March 1945 in Burma. He was 21 years old. His grave is at Taukkyan War Cemetery, Htauk Kyant, Yangon Region, Burma. His death was only three weeks before VE day, although the surrender in the Far East did not come until August 1945.

The ABC firm must have carried on with Peter and Percival Clarence Hewson running it. In June 1948 Percival filed a patent application entitled 'Improvements in or relating to awnings, sun blinds and the like'. It has much detail of cables, tensioning wires, reduction of sagging, laths and brackets. It appears that the patent, number 643624, was granted in September 1950.

If my research is correct Elsie died in 1979 aged 90. Peter died in 2009, also aged 90. They were both long lived, and it would be marvellous to discover that Peter has some living descendants.

Chapter 24

Rose Adelaide Blenkarn
(first cousin three times removed)

ROSE WAS THE fifth child and third daughter of Alfred Bower Blenkarn and Mary Ann (née Page). She was born in 1858, the day after her maternal grandmother died. When she was three years old her Aunt Adelaide was living with her family. Grandfather Samuel Page had died in 1860 and Mary Ann took in her younger sister Adelaide for a while, before she moved in with her sister Eliza and then her brother Samuel the Younger.

In 1871 Rose was at Osborne House School in Clapham, a boarding school for girls aged 12-16. By this time, her elder sister Marianne was training to become a governess. In 1878 her sister Alice married Herbert Platt, who was an accountant. Rose's mother died in 1879. In the 1881 census Rose was living with her father on Darville Road in Hackney. Alfred's occupation is paper merchant. There is no trace of Rose at the 1891 census, although her father was lodging with a widow in St Helier, Jersey.

In June 1892 she was in London, witnessing her sister Marianne's wedding to Edmund Hussey Lough Taylor at St Philips Church, Dalston, Hackney. Her Aunt Adelaide was the other witness to the marriage. Edmund, a merchant's clerk was 41 and Marianne gave her age as 41, although she was actually 43. Perhaps she didn't want to acknowledge that Edmund was two years her junior. She was still a governess. Edmund's mother, Charlotte Hussey, was a sister of Frances Hussey, who was married to my great-great-grandfather, William Augustus Page. Therefore Frances was an aunt to Edmund through his mother. Frances was also an aunt to Marianne, as William Augustus was the younger brother of Mary Ann, Marianne's mother. I guess that Marianne and Edmund were quasi cousins through marriage but were not directly related.

Meanwhile her brothers, Alfred Elston and William Chalmers had both married. Alfred and his wife Annie, née Peart, moved to Australia and had six children. William Chalmers was married twice, to Julia Wilkinson and Florence Bennett and there is something a bit mysterious about him. His divorce papers (which can be seen online) state that he did not have any children, but he had three at that time. In total he had three sons and a daughter. Two of the sons went to New Zealand and there are probably still Blenkarn descendants there and in Australia to this day.

In October 1900, Rose was the recipient of one of Aunt Adelaide's shares of Section 8 Goodwood, and she also received, as did Arthur Claud Page, a half-share of the residuary amount of her aunt's estate. So, Rose would have been well off, perhaps for the first time in her life. In 1901 she was still living in Hackney on Lower Clapton Road. She is listed as working on her own account as a confectioner. It could be that she was able to use some of Aunt Adelaide's inheritance to set herself up in business. Also living with her was a lodger called Rudolf Kranhaus, a civil engineer aged 24. Despite his Germanic sounding name the census records that he was born in London.

Her father, the architect, merchant, paper merchant, shipping broker but mostly fraudster, died in Camberwell in the second quarter of 1901. He left no Will and judging by his lifestyle I doubt that he had anything to leave.

In 1911 Rose moved south of the River Thames to 8A Stanford Parade, London Road, Norbury, Surrey. There is no mention of the confectionery business; her occupation states 'private means'. Her property was a six-roomed dwelling. Kitchens counted as one room, but bathrooms were not included. It probably had a kitchen, dining room, living room and three bedrooms. Also, still living with her was Rudolf Kranhaus, aged 34 and his occupation is now phosphate agent's clerk. Rose was 53. It seems extraordinary that a 'lodger' should move house with his landlady. Could there have been more to this relationship? Did Rose have a toy boy?

Unlike her father who always seemed to be in court or the bankruptcy court, Rose lived a blameless life – sadly without leaving traces. The only information available is from official records of birth, marriage, census or electoral registers and inevitably death. Rose wasn't married, so information about her is even more limited. Both her sisters pre-deceased her; both died in March 1932, which must have been a sad blow for Rose. Her brothers hadn't been long-lived, Alfred dying in 1903, only two years after his father, and William in 1916.

Rose lived for 80 years and died on 22nd October 1938. I have found that most of the Wills left by women are very detailed about the household minutiae and it is this that reveals the character of the person. Rose wrote her Will in 1919, so soon after she had received her 1/6th share of Goodwood Section 8. She appointed her nephew, Alice's son, Herbert, as her Executor and Trustee and she left him £100. To her six nieces and nephews in Australia, her brother Alfred's children, she left £200 each. There were also three great-nieces and a great-nephew in Australia, who each received £50.

There were several bequests of jewellery, her gramophone and various quilts and counterpanes to her friends Margaret Elizabeth Huebscher, Rose Turner, Mabel Crowhurst and her husband George. To her dear niece Rosa Platt, wife of Herbert, she leaves all her plate and linen, the work box left to her by her aunt, her gold watch and chain and the sum of £50. To Rose and Herbert's daughter Joan Rosa Platt she leaves her watch bracelet and £50.

Her sisters Marianne and Alice were to receive all her personal wardrobe, carpets, curtains and rugs. Marianne was also to receive the income from Rose's £1,200 investment in War Loan. She requests that Abney Park Cemetery Company be paid £25 to keep the family grave for 25 years. She also desired that not more than £40 be expended on her funeral. She left the residue of her estate to her sisters. However, they both died before Rose so in that case she desired that the whole income arising from her estate should go to her nephew Herbert Platt.

Rose added a Codicil to her Will in 1921 to bequeath £50 to Cecil Blenkarn in New Zealand and £50 to his son Kenneth. Also, the Cripple Home carried on by Sir William Treloar was to receive £50. Probate was granted on the 18th November 1938 and her estate was valued at £8,160. Rose was buried at Abney Park Cemetery in plot 8SO2 and her father is in plot 4S12.

Her nephew Herbert Platt, like his father an accountant, who inherited the income from her estate died in 1963. His executrix was his daughter Joan Adelaide Rosa King (née Platt). Herbert and his wife had lived in Cockfosters, Hertfordshire. Probate was granted to Joan King in July 1963, valued at £89,213. Joan had been married twice, firstly to John Ives and then to Herbert S King. I do not have any record of children born within either marriage. Joan died in 1983.

The trail for the inheritance of Section 8 Goodwood had once again gone cold.

Chapter 25

Rose Phyllis Maude Newnham
(no relation)

FINALLY, I COME to the last recipient of a one-sixth share of Goodwood Section 8. Thanks to great-great-great-aunt Eliza leaving her share out of the family to Rose Phyllis Maude Newnham I have spent many hours trying to pin down this non-relative. It has been like plaiting fog!

There is something mysterious about Rose. The affidavit signed by her father when she was in India gives her date of birth as 12th April 1891. He also states that she was born in Bristol. This information is confirmed in the 1901 and 1939 censuses. However, there is absolutely no record of the birth of a child of this name in Bristol.

Rose's father was Charles Edward Newnham. He was a solicitor, living in Doughty Street London, where Aunt Eliza lived. He later moved to Walton-on-Thames and thence to Ringwood in Hampshire. Charles had been born in Ahmedabad in India, within the Bombay Residency, on 22nd February 1863. His father was William Huertly Newnham who was in the Bombay Civil Service. William's wife, Charles' mother, was Agnes Louisa Caroline Newnham.

Charles Newnham married Elizabeth Agnes Roberts in St Pancras, London, in the first quarter of 1892. Interestingly, Rose was born the year before her parents were married. Nothing wrong with that, but curious in that day and age. There is no indication of Charles or Elizabeth having lived in Bristol. Children, more often than not, were given at least one of the names of their parents. Rose Phyllis Maude – none of these names are from her 'mother' nor her Newnham grandmother. Various thoughts and options came to mind. Could she be an illegitimate child of Charles, who then took care of her when he married Elizabeth? Was she the child of a relative who had died, and they adopted her? Was she the illegitimate child of Elizabeth? Reluctantly, I have to conclude that there is no answer.

Charles and Elizabeth had a daughter, Agnes Muriel born in 1893 and then a son, Horace Claude Charles who was born on 28th October 1896. This child was baptised at Holy Trinity, Gray's Inn Road, on 22nd October 1897, so he was nearly a year old. His parents were living at 53 Doughty Street. It was good to see this information as it confirmed that they lived either next door, or across the street from Aunt Eliza.

Whatever Rose's origins she obviously made a major impression upon Aunt Eliza. She was the main beneficiary of Eliza's Will. It is not difficult to imagine a lonely, childless elderly woman being enchanted by this little girl and her younger sister and brother. The feelings for these children may have been enhanced by the fact that their mother Elizabeth died in July 1898, when they were very young. Possibly the childless Eliza felt that she could be of use and help to these three motherless children. After all, apart from her sister Adelaide, all her siblings had families of their own and she probably never felt very 'needed'. However, Eliza was in her late sixties and George had died in 1891, so whatever relationship there was between Eliza and the Newnhams is unknown. In the 1901 census Charles Newnham and his three children had moved from Doughty Street, to Walton-on-Thames, in Surrey, where they were looked after by a housekeeper and a nursemaid.

Eliza died in 1906 when Rose was about 15 years old. Rose received various personal artefacts from Eliza, as listed in the chapter about Eliza, but, most important financially was the share of the land in Adelaide. However, at the time of Eliza's death there was no indication that the court case would ever be resolved, nor what the value would be.

In 1908 Charles married again. Grace was the new Mrs Newnham, and in due course they moved to Netheravon, Ringwood, Hampshire. In the 1911 census I can see that this was a nine-roomed house and they had one general servant. Agnes Muriel was now 18 years old. Horace Claude Charles was a pupil at Lancing College at Steyning in Sussex. But where was Rose?

Rose's father had been born in India. Her paternal grandfather had been in the Indian Civil Service. Her father's brother, Arthur Newnham was a Colonel in the army based at Jullundur Cantonment in the Punjab in India. Girls belonging to the 'class' that Charles occupied, that is professional and with Indian connections, were known as the 'fishing fleet'. In other words, they sailed off to India in search of a husband. So many Englishmen of their class were running the British Empire, in the Army, the Civil Service or business, that there were probably more eligible men in India than in England.

So, Rose's Uncle Arthur was providing a home for her in India and no doubt she enjoyed a whirl of parties, picnics, dances and dinners and possibly tiger hunts with the young officers of his regiment. It would have been very reminiscent of 'Jewel in the Crown', 'Passage to India' and books by Kipling. I'm sure she got to know many people of her own age, because Uncle Arthur and Aunt Ekaterina had a son, Lance, who was also in the army and was two years older than Rose. Arthur met Ekaterina when he was the military attaché to the court of Tsar Nicholas. They then moved with the Russians to India. Jullunder is now written as Jalandhar and the cantonment looks very similar to the one at Quetta where my great-grandfather was stationed. When I was looking up the location of this cantonment in the Punjab, I found information about Rose's cousin, Colonel Lance Newnham. He was awarded the Military Cross in WW1 and finished the war in the rank of Brigadier General.

At the start of WW2, he was serving with the British Army Aid Group in British Hong Kong. He was taken prisoner when the Japanese invaded Hong Kong in December 1941 and, with two other officers, worked to contact British agents and organise a mass escape. The Japanese discovered the plan and arrested the trio, torturing them in Stanley Prison to gain more information. They refused to divulge any further names despite being beaten, starved and threatened with death. They were killed by firing squad in Sham Shui Prison Camp on 18 December 1943. Lance is buried at the Stanley Military Cemetery in Hong Kong.

He was awarded the George Cross posthumously and it was presented to his widow Phyllis (who had herself been interned by the Japanese) and son Claude by King George VI at Buckingham Palace on 3rd December 1946. His many medals are on display in the Ashcroft Gallery at the Imperial War Museum.

During 1910 and 1911 Rose would have had many dancing partners and enjoyed a great social life. In those days before two devastating world wars, she and her cousin Lance would have been young and relatively carefree. It wasn't very long before Rose's mission was accomplished. Her marriage was announced in the 20th October edition of *The Times of India*.

> Rose Phyllis Maude Newnham married on 4th October 1911 to Alfred H Peyton at Christ Church, Mussoorie, Uttaran-chal, India.

Rose was 20 and Arthur was an army officer and a widower, aged 29. Mussoorie was a beautiful hill station not too far from Dehradun and south east of Shimla. I expect they made their home there and moved whenever the Army directed.

In due course two children were born. Molly Norah Peyton arrived in 1913 and Henry Newnham Peyton in 1915. In 1924 Rose and her children arrived in Plymouth aboard the ship *City of Nagpur* from Karachi. She was going to stay with her father and his wife at Broadshard House, Ringwood. I also wonder if she was going to leave the children in England to go to school. This was the usual pattern for parents stationed in India. The children came to England and if they were lucky kind relatives took care of them in the holidays, as parents usually only got leave every two years. I think that this must have happened because in 1926 Rose is travelling alone from Bombay on the P&O liner *Rawalpindi* bound for London. This formed the pattern for the next few years, with Rose travelling alone. However, in 1930 Arthur is with her on the P&O ship *Ranpura* enroute from Bombay to London. Again, in 1933, she and Arthur have come through the Suez Canal aboard a Netherlands Royal Mail ship on their way to Southampton.

In 1933 Arthur would have been 50, which may have been retirement age from the Army, and there are no more voyages to and from India listed. Her father died in 1935 in Bournemouth, although his and Grace's home was still at Ringwood. Rose and Arthur's daughter Molly was married in 1937 to Charles W H Rice and their son Henry married Margaret Moser in 1940 in London. The 1939 census records Rose and Arthur living at 7 Stanley Avenue, Beckenham, Kent. Arthur Henry is noted as being a retired Colonel in the Indian Army. Rose was an unpaid ARP (Air Raid Protection) warden in Beckenham. Good for Rose! They then moved to Ipswich in Suffolk; perhaps it was a safer place, during the war, or maybe they moved afterwards. Arthur died there at the East Suffolk and Ipswich Hospital on the 30th April 1950.

Rose was 59 years old and a couple of years later in September 1952 she married again, to Geoffrey William Dawson. Whether Geoffrey was wealthy, or now that her children were married, it seems that she definitely got the travel bug. In 1953 they went on a round trip to Africa on the *Rhodesia Castle*. In 1955 they spent many months travelling. In January they sailed to Canada, returning via Florida. Just before Christmas that year they set off for Fremantle, Australia, returning via Sri Lanka (then still Ceylon) arriving back in Southampton at the end of February. Their residence was 7 Colneis Road, Felixstowe in Suffolk. In December 1957 they were off again; this time on a round voyage to Yokohama Japan, on the P&O ship *Chusan*, arriving back in London three months later. I wonder if they called at Hong Kong and if she visited her cousin Lance's grave.

Vancouver, Seattle and San Francisco were their venues in January 1960, returning in April. It occurs to me that they were nearly always away at Christmas time. If there are grandchildren that is the time you usually want to be with them. Were either her son or daughter based overseas with children? It's possible.

The 1960 voyage seems to be the last recorded trip. Her husband Geoffrey died in March 1969 at Samford, in Suffolk. Rose herself died on 13th January 1977, aged 85 in the Brierfield Retirement Home at Trimley St Mary, Ipswich. Wills listed online since the 1970s do not show who probate was granted to, but she left £52,369, which would have the equivalent purchasing power in £400K in 2018. I do not know whether she has any living relatives.

Epilogue

IN JANUARY 2018 I received the results of my DNA test, via
Ancestry.com. It confirmed that I was primarily English, Scottish, Irish, with a smattering of Swedish and French. This is
probably the case for many British people whose family has
always lived in the UK.

In addition to the analysis of my DNA profile I was sent a long
list of 3rd, 4th, 5th and more distant cousins. Some 220 in total.
Many on the list did not have a family tree attached to them, i.e.
they had not used Ancestry for researching their history, they just
had their DNA analysed. I certainly did not have the wish to
contact all these people to find out how, or even if, we were related.

Scanning down the list I saw some distant Australian cousins
related through my mother's side of the family and who I had
been in contact with via Ancestry, over the past few years. It felt
good to know that the DNA matching system worked. Then I came
across a familiar surname, Catherine Page. My heart skipped a
beat. Other than my immediate first cousins in the UK I had no
knowledge of living Page relatives. However, there was no family
tree attached, so I could not verify the relationship. I decided to
send a message to this Catherine Page, with a brief outline of my
family line to establish where she might fit in. I received the
following response from her:

> "Hi Penny, having recently received my Ancestry DNA
> results I'm amazed and overwhelmed by the number of
> relatives I have been matched with. As my father, Hugh
> Page, his brother John and their parents John, known as
> Jack, and his mother Joyce, have all passed away, my

knowledge is very limited. I'm attempting to start my family tree. When I'm a little further down the track with this project I'll have some idea of my relatives and I'll be in touch. Thank you for getting in touch with me. Kind regards, Catherine Hunt née Page".

It was kind of Catherine to reply but I was slightly disappointed that she didn't seem to share my excitement at finding a distant relative. I started to look on my family tree to see whether her grandparents featured on it. Living relatives are not shown on Ancestry and it is quite difficult to even locate birth details for relatives born after 1950. I found her grandfather, John Page. His father was Francis Page, son of Adam Kirkaldy Page, who lived in Merimbula, New South Wales and had arrived in Australia in 1853. I was quite ecstatic to then realise that Catherine and I were fourth cousins, and that Samuel Page was three times great-grandfather to both of us.

This was a real find. I wrote back to her explaining who I was in relation to her. Back came her reply that she knew almost nothing about her Page heritage, but she would like to know more. She lived in New South Wales, Australia. Catherine, you were a dream come true! Most of my family had become bored with hearing me talk about various distant relatives. But here was a cousin, who despite my initial reaction, was incredibly interested to hear about her forebears. I needed no additional encouragement. I told Catherine I would tell her the story of Samuel Page and his land in Adelaide so that she would know more about the Page family. I began with almost weekly instalments. It was a delight to be able to recount the story. I had so often thought that I would like to write a book about the Adelaide court case and the beginnings of the butter business and all the associated happenings that I had traced about the Page family.

My initial impressions about Catherine's enthusiasm were absolutely unfounded. She was the 'dream audience' that every writer would like to have. Her enthusiasm for what I had written, and her constant support and encouragement kept me going. She told me that reading the story was like watching a 'mini-series'. Before long I realised that I more or less had the outline of a book, and the story just 'grew like Topsy'. You have just read it.

I am indebted to Catherine, a very warm and big-hearted cousin, whom I hope to meet one day. I dedicate *A Book full of Pages* to you, Catherine.

Acknowledgements

I offer my grateful thanks to Graham Jaunay of Proformat in Adelaide and Pat Raymond of the Bega Genealogical Society for their expertise and assistance in my research in Australia.

John Eastberg, Director of the Pabst Museum, Milwaukee furnished me with a copy of the painting donated to the Layton Art Gallery by Samuel Page and also sent me a copy of Samuel's signature. His book on the history of Layton's gallery is a tour de force and I quoted Layton's niece from this book.

I have received encouragement from my children and grand-children, other family members and many friends over the years and I thank them for their patience and fortitude and for not rolling their eyes too much, when I started relating details of great, great, greats....

Ancestry is a marvellous source of material and several people have been able to confirm queries that I have had. I have also struck up long distance relationships with various people who are in some way related through me or my late husband, who have been invaluable in my family history research. In no particular order my thanks for help and enthusiasm are due to:

Duncan Briggs, in the US, related to Robert Denny Briggs and Harry Robert Briggs.

Paul Field in NSW who is probably distantly related via Frances Page (née Hussey).

Penny Stewart in Australia whose husband is a distant relative of Rose Phyllis Maud Newnham's second husband.

Glenda Mitchell, Simon and Diane Newton, Jean Newbiggin and Jennifer Bonham, in Australia and the UK, for help and encouragement on research into other branches of my family.

Christine Gill in New Zealand who is distantly related to Roy and Mason Gill.

The newspaper archive in Find My Past has been well utilised, as has *Trove*, the free online newspaper archive in Australia.

The attendees at Joanna Moorhead's 'Writing your family history' course told me that my story was worth recording and that I should visit Adelaide.

Thanks to Jane Frost 'Frostie' for her excellent company on my weekend in Sydney and for being the only person that I know who has also been on holiday to Å in the Lofoten Islands.

I'm very glad that Adam and Debbie Bough emigrated to Adelaide – it was so good to make friends when I was a long way from home.

Thanks also to three people who are no longer with me, but whose love, support and encouragement I really appreciated; my parents Doug and Beth Page and my darling Jeff, who is very much missed.

Appendix

City of Freedom Archives

People Who Had To Be Free

Many people assume that the Freedom of the City of London is purely an honorary award, presented only to the great and the good, or for particular bravery, for example. However, this is true of only a very small number of City Freemen. The Honorary Freedom of the City of London is indeed the highest honour that the City can bestow, but it is granted very rarely. The vast majority of City Freemen were, and are, admitted by other means, and represent a very broad cross-section of the population. Over the last 300 years, about 300,000 ordinary people have been made Free of the City of London. Even today, many men and women continue to be admitted to the City Freedom, although most of the privileges and practical reasons for doing so have now disappeared.

Before the mid-19th century, the Freedom of the City of London was a practical necessity for those who plied a trade or made their living in the City of London. Indeed, certain groups of people were compelled, on pain of prosecution, to be Free of the City, including:

- Common Councilmen, Aldermen (including the Lord Mayor) and Sheriffs of the City (all still must be Free of the City today);
- Liverymen of the City Livery Companies (all still must be Free of the City today);

- Most City of London Corporation employees (this lasted until well into the 20th century, particularly for higher grades of staff);
- Retail traders within the City (until the 1850s);
- City "sworn" or licensed brokers (until 1853)
- Licensed victuallers in the City of London (until 1853);
- Journeymen employees of City Freemen within the City of London, although, under an Act of Common Council of 1750, non-free journeymen could be employed if the master obtained a licence from the City of London Corporation.

Many other people chose to become Free of the City because of the privileges it carried with it, or for reasons of their own. However, some of those who ought to have been Free often evaded it, on grounds of cost or principle, and some were prosecuted for this.

Rights and Privileges

Historically, only City Freemen could:
- vote in Parliamentary elections;
- vote in civic elections, for each Ward's Common Councilmen and Alderman;
- be exempt from all tolls payable on animals brought into the City for sale;
- be exempt from all market tolls payable anywhere in the country;
- be exempt from naval impressment;
- enjoy certain legal privileges with respect to being tried and imprisoned.

All of these historic privileges are now defunct although, even today, the City Freedom continues to be a necessary qualification for certain civic offices (see People who had to be Free above).

Contrary to popular belief, City Freemen do not have the right to herd sheep, or animals of any kind over London Bridge, or any other bridges, although this belief probably stems from the

Freemen's historic exemption from tolls on animals brought into the City for sale. There are several other popular myths about some so-called privileges of City Freemen which are equally false, and which are de-bunked in Caroline Arnold's book (see Further Reading, below).

Qualifications

In order to be Free of the City, a person has to be:

- historically, over 21 years of age. However, the age of admission was lowered by Act of Common Council of 6 November 2008 to 18 years of age
- historically, a British or Commonwealth subject by birth or naturalisation (this requirement was dropped for citizens of the European Union in 1996, and for other non-Britons in 1999). Formerly, foreign dignitaries were sometimes voted the honorary Freedom, and given an address of welcome in the Guildhall. However, most could not make the Freeman's declaration of allegiance to the British Crown in the form in which it was required of all Freemen before 1996, and so could not technically be Freemen.

Both men and women have always been able to be Free, although married women have only been admissible since 1923. Before then, a Free spinster or widow who subsequently married lost her Freedom during her marriage. A non-free widow of a City Freeman obtained the Freedom herself "by courtesy" on her husband's death, so that she could continue his business. However, such widows were not formally admitted to the Freedom, and so there are no records of them. Women who were Free of the City used to be known as "Free Sisters", a term now only maintained by some of the City Livery Companies for their own female Freemen.

Members of the Society of Friends (Quakers) were legally permitted to make an affirmation on admission in place of the Freeman's oath from 1696, and their City Freedom admission papers were usually marked with a "Q". Jewish and other non-Christian British subjects were allowed to be admitted to the City Freedom after 1830, although some Jewish Freemen were also admitted before 1738.

Before 1835, every person who wished to become a City Freeman first had to become a Freeman of one of the City Livery Companies (as the successors to the medieval trade and craft guilds are known). The Freedom, or ordinary membership, of a Livery Company, is a separate Freedom from the Freedom of the City. A person wishing to become a Liveryman (i.e. a senior member) of a Livery Company must first be a Freeman both of that Company and of the City of London. A person who is a Freeman of both the City and a Livery Company is referred to as "Citizen and [Livery Company name] of London".

People can belong to more than one City Livery Company, in which case one Company, usually the first one joined, is known as the person's Mother Company. It was fairly uncommon for a person to belong to more than one Livery Company before the 19th century.

Over the centuries, some Livery Companies lost their original trade or craft links, and so it is not at all safe to assume that someone in a Company followed the occupation of that Company: a "Citizen and Spectacle maker of London" would not necessarily have been a working optician, for example.

Ways of being Admitted

There are four ways of becoming a Freeman, each of which can be undertaken either through, or without, the intervention of one of the Livery Companies (although before 1835, one had to be a Livery Company member first):

The Honorary Freedom, the highest honour the City of London Corporation can bestow, which is granted only by special Resolution of the Court of Common Council to distinguished and worthy people, either as individuals (e.g. Winston Churchill, Florence

Nightingale) or as members of particular groups (e.g. the City Imperial Volunteers in the Boer War, the City Fire-Watchers in the 2nd World War);

Servitude, by which a person has to complete an apprenticeship of at least 7 (or, since 1889, 4) years' duration to a City Freeman;

Patrimony, open only to the legitimate and natural children of a male (or, since 1976, female) Freeman who were born after their parent's own Freedom admission. Since 1999, adopted children and children legitimated by the subsequent marriage of their parents have also been eligible for admission by patrimony, so long as their birth date was after the City Freedom admission of their adopter or parent;

Redemption, or purchase, obtainable by any one of the following ways:

- Presentation by an officer of the City of London Corporation or other person who had been granted the right of presenting a limited number of candidates in lieu of salary or as a reward for services or as a means of raising revenue by the City of London Corporation. The intending Freeman usually had to pay the officer for presenting him or her, in addition to the usual Freedom fees, although the City Freedom archives do not note this personal fee. This right was abolished in the mid-19th century;
- Directly petitioning the Court of Aldermen, if becoming Free through the intervention of a City Livery Company;
- Directly petitioning the Court of Common Council, if no Livery Company were involved (possible after 1835 only);

By being on the City Parliamentary Register of Electors (possible after 1856 only).

Further Reading

My Ancestors Were Freemen of the City of London by Vivienne E. Aldous (Society of Genealogists, 1999), concentrates particularly on the historic City Freedom admission papers, and the information contained in them which is likely to be useful to family historians.

Sheep Over London Bridge: The Freedom of the City of London, by Caroline Arnold (Corporation of London, 2nd edition 2001), is a popular guide to the City Freedom generally, including the present-day admission procedures in a City of London context.

The Chamberlain of the City of London, 1237-1987, by Betty R. Masters, (Corporation of London, 1988 [out of print]), especially Chapter 8, 'The Chamberlain's Court: Freedom and Apprenticeship'. This is a scholarly but readable book about the whole history and function of the Chamberlain of London from the Middle Ages, including his jurisdiction over City apprentices and Freemen.

Bibliography

Title	Author	Publisher
Colonial Sketches	Robert Harrison	Hall, Virtue & Co
The Fatal Shore	Robert Hughes	Vintage
History of the City of Adelaide	Thomas Worsnop	Kessinger Legacy Reprints
My experiences in Australia 1856-7	A Lady (Emma Macpherson)	Dodo Press
The Story of Adelaide	The Queen Adelaide Society	
Proposal to His Majesty's Government for founding a colony on the Southern Coast of Australia	South Australian Land Company	Forgotten Books
1850 A very good year in the Colony of South Australia	Russell Smith	Shakespeare Head Press
Private Journal of a Voyage to Australia – 1839	James Bell	
The Stag Diary – Passage to Colonial Adelaide – 1850	Doug Limbrick	
A Private Empire	Stephen Foster	Pier 9
The Narrow Road to the Deep North	Richard Flanagan	Vintage
The Fishing Fleet –Husband hunting in the Raj	Anne de Courcy	Phoenix

Family Trees

The Scott Family
The Page and Retemeyer Cousins
Samuel Page 1796-1860

The Scott Family History

Showing descendents from George Scott (1735-1791) to 2014, including all Page children, some of their offspring (those mentioned in the book), and identifying the recipients of the shares of Section 8 Goodwood, Adelaide.

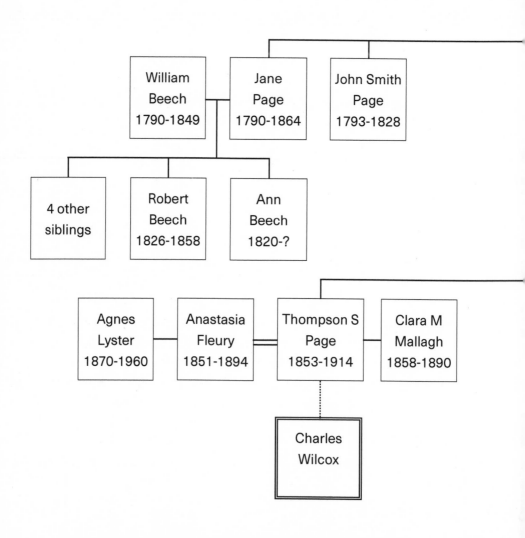

Those shown within these bounded boxes were recipients of the proceeds of the sale of Section 8 Goodwood, Adelaide.

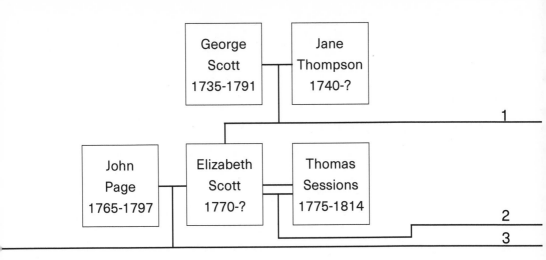

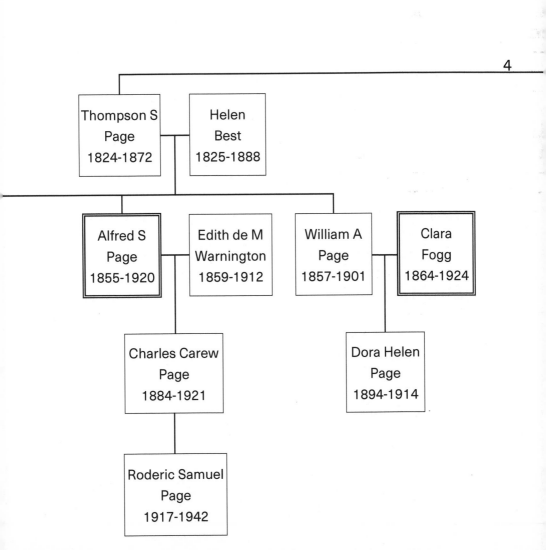

1 _____

2 _____
3 _____

4 _____

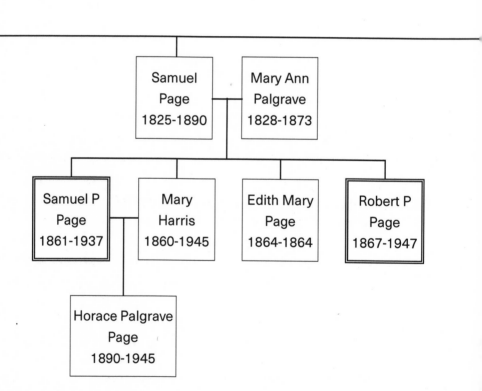

| Samuel Page 1825-1890 | Mary Ann Palgrave 1828-1873 |

| Samuel P Page 1861-1937 | Mary Harris 1860-1945 | Edith Mary Page 1864-1864 | Robert P Page 1867-1947 |

Horace Palgrave Page 1890-1945

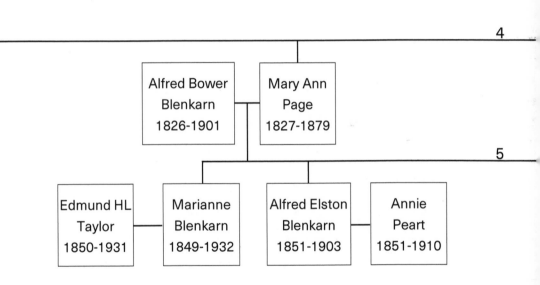

1

2

3

4

Alfred Bower
Blenkarn
1826-1901

Mary Ann
Page
1827-1879

5

Edmund HL
Taylor
1850-1931

Marianne
Blenkarn
1849-1932

Alfred Elston
Blenkarn
1851-1903

Annie
Peart
1851-1910

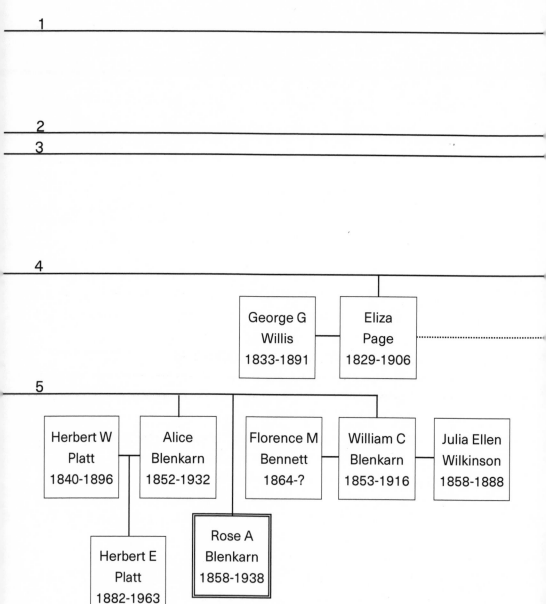

1

2

3

4

| George G Willis 1833-1891 | Eliza Page 1829-1906 |

5

| Herbert W Platt 1840-1896 | Alice Blenkarn 1852-1932 | Florence M Bennett 1864-? | William C Blenkarn 1853-1916 | Julia Ellen Wilkinson 1858-1888 |

| Herbert E Platt 1882-1963 | Rose A Blenkarn 1858-1938 |

| Joan Adelaide Rose Platt 1912-1983 |

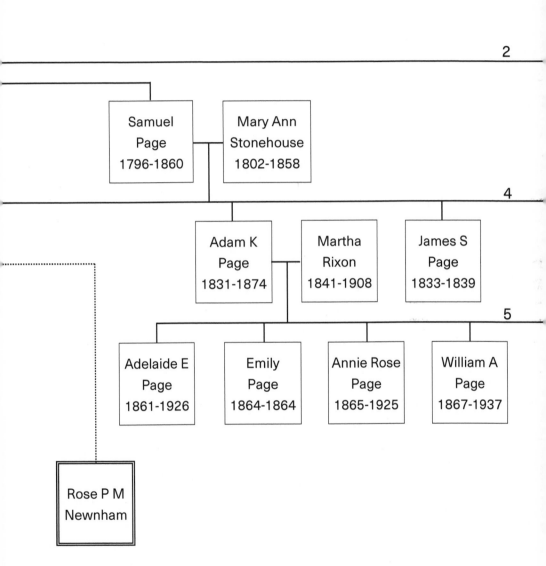

1

2

Samuel
Page
1796-1860

Mary Ann
Stonehouse
1802-1858

4

Adam K
Page
1831-1874

Martha
Rixon
1841-1908

James S
Page
1833-1839

5

Adelaide E
Page
1861-1926

Emily
Page
1864-1864

Annie Rose
Page
1865-1925

William A
Page
1867-1937

Rose P M
Newnham

1 ———————————————————————————————————————

2 ———————————————————————————————————————

4 ———————————————————————————————————————

5 ———————————————————————————————————————

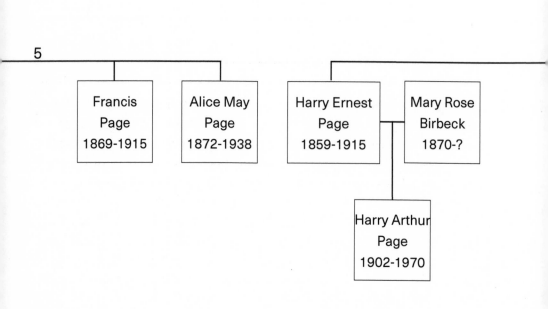

| Francis Page 1869-1915 | Alice May Page 1872-1938 | Harry Ernest Page 1859-1915 | Mary Rose Birbeck 1870-? |

Harry Arthur Page 1902-1970

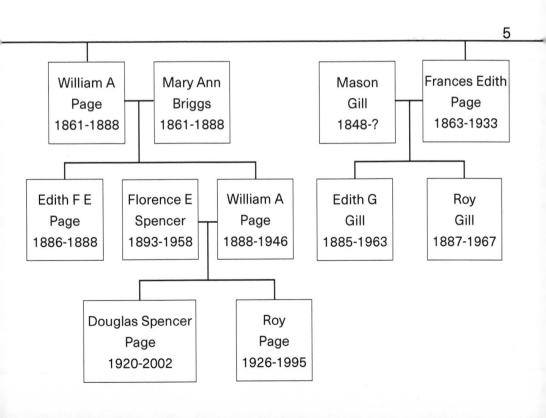

1

2

4

5

| William A Page 1861-1888 | Mary Ann Briggs 1861-1888 | | Mason Gill 1848-? | Frances Edith Page 1863-1933 |

Edith F E Page 1886-1888

Florence E Spencer 1893-1958

William A Page 1888-1946

Edith G Gill 1885-1963

Roy Gill 1887-1967

Douglas Spencer Page 1920-2002

Roy Page 1926-1995

1

2

4

William A Page 1836-1896	Frances Hussey 1840-1918	Adelaide Page 1838-1900

5

Clarence K Page 1864-1915	Stanley E Page 1867-1938	George Henry Bond 1876-1964	Kathleen O Page 1867-1968

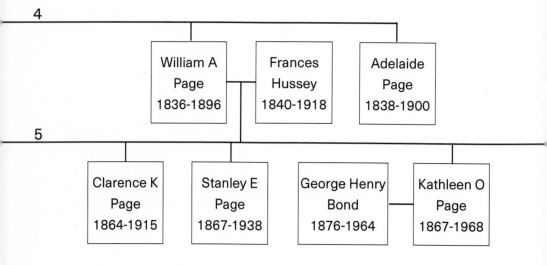

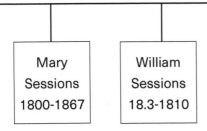

| Mary Sessions 1800-1867 | William Sessions 18.3-1810 |

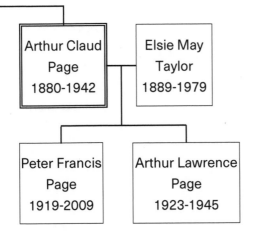

| Arthur Claud Page 1880-1942 | Elsie May Taylor 1889-1979 |

| Peter Francis Page 1919-2009 | Arthur Lawrence Page 1923-1945 |

1

2

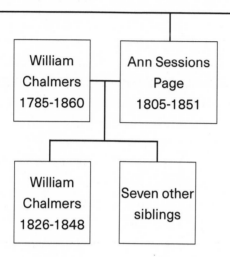

William
Chalmers
1785-1860

Ann Sessions
Page
1805-1851

William
Chalmers
1826-1848

Seven other
siblings

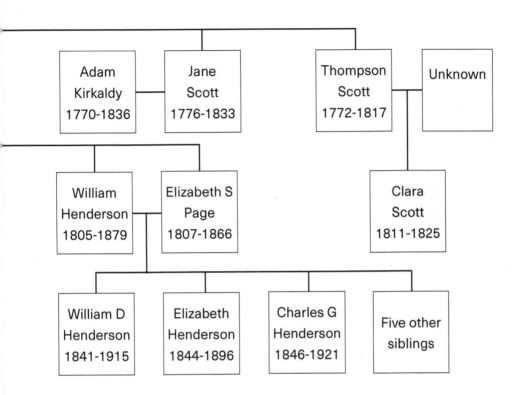

The Page and Retemeyer Cousins

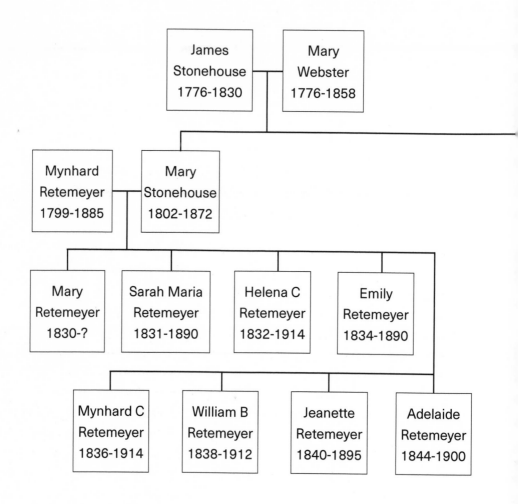

Note:

Mary Ann and Mary Stonehouse were twins, who married Samuel Page and Mynhard Retemeyer.

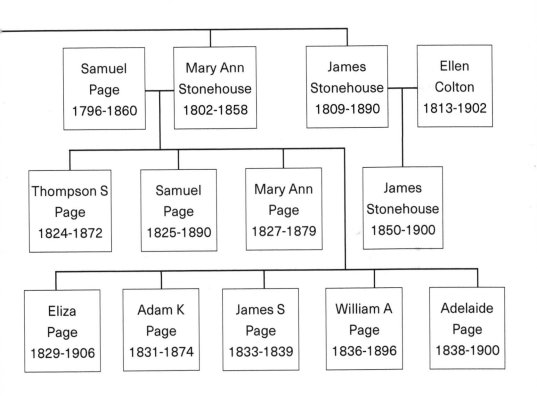

Samuel Page 1796-1860

Showing his siblings and half-siblings

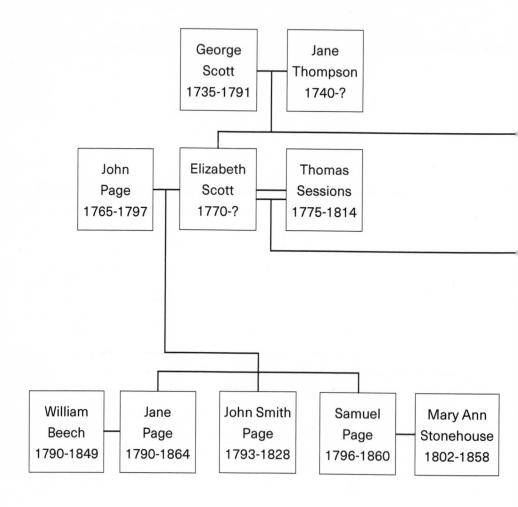

| George Scott 1735-1791 | Jane Thompson 1740-? |

| John Page 1765-1797 | Elizabeth Scott 1770-? | Thomas Sessions 1775-1814 |

| William Beech 1790-1849 | Jane Page 1790-1864 | John Smith Page 1793-1828 | Samuel Page 1796-1860 | Mary Ann Stonehouse 1802-1858 |

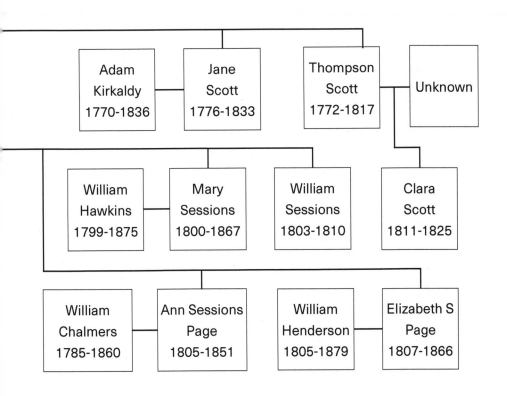